Conjectures
and Refutations
in Syntax and Semantics

STUDIES IN LINGUISTIC ANALYSIS

Editors
**Noam Chomsky, Joan W. Bresnan,
and Michael K. Brame**

Conjectures
and Refutations
in Syntax and Semantics

Michael K. Brame
University of Washington

North-Holland
PUBLISHING COMPANY
NEW YORK · AMSTERDAM

American Elsevier Publishing Company, Inc.
52 Vanderbilt Avenue, New York, NY 10017

North-Holland Publishing Company
P.O. Box 211
Amsterdam, The Netherlands

Library of Congress Cataloging in Publication Data

Brame, Michael K   1944—
Conjectures and refutations in syntax and semantics.

(Studies in linguistic analysis series)
Bibliography: p.
Includes index.
1. Semantics—Addresses, essays, lectures. 2. Gen-
erative grammar—Addresses, essays, lectures. 3. Gram-
mar, Comparative and general—Syntax—Addresses, essays,
lectures. I. Title.
P325.B68   415   75—39767
ISBN 0—7204—8604—1   North-Holland
ISBN 0—444—00185—9   American Elsevier

Manufactured in the United States of America

for the inmates of 200 Biltstraat

Contents

Preface

I had the good fortune of spending the 1973–74 academic year at the Instituut voor Algemene Taalwetenschap of the Rijksuniversiteit te Utrecht, as a Fulbright-Hays lecturer. Approximately one half of the lectures delivered during my tenure there I devoted to controversial themes in current linguistic syntax and semantics. The other half I devoted to current issues in generative phonology. The lectures printed here deal with syntax and semantics and reflect fairly accurately the content of the lectures as originally conceived. I have nevertheless expanded some portions of the original 1973 manuscript and excised others. The order of presentation here also differs from that of the oral presentation.

The opening lecture sets the ensuing discussion in historical perspective, although it is to be noted that my view of the history of modern linguistics is at odds with all interpretations of which I am aware.

In the lectures of Part I of this collection, I have scrutinized and criticized generative semantics, delineating what I consider to be the major issues dividing the generative semantics camp and that of the standard theory. Here I have drawn on much of the refutational literature to build my case. For example, I have appropriated some of the criticism of generative semantics found in [24], which is also my source for the apropos quote of Frege introducing Chapter 3. Although my discussion does not exhaust the arguments that can be leveled against generative semantics, I do think it is fairly comprehensive and representative of the point of view adopted by advocates of the standard theory of generative grammar.

There will be those who no longer consider generative semantics an issue worthy of serious debate. This was not so much the case in 1971–72 when these lectures were conceived as now in 1975 when these pages go to press. Such readers could turn directly to Part II, where the (extended) standard theory is confronted, but they, too, may find something of interest in Part I.

In Part II I have focused attention on the putative rule of Equi-NP Deletion, subjected it to a critical reevaluation, and ultimately rejected it.

Two alternatives to the standard theory are outlined in the closing lecture. Lest I give the wrong impression, I hasten to point out that my "alternatives" to the standard theory could be viewed as extensions or elaborations of the existing theory of transformational grammar, whereas this is not so in the case of generative semantics (for the reasons offered in Part I).

The contrast between Parts I and II will be evident throughout. In Part I, a certain approach to the study of natural language is rejected. In Part II, a certain approach is accepted and certain aspects of that approach criticized and rejected. Besides the fact that these two parts made up my Fulbright-Hays lectures in syntax and semantics, there is a reason for collecting them in one volume. The unifying theme which I want to emphasize is this: A new perspective can often be approached and better analyses broached through a critical reexamination of current proposals. In this sense, the volume could well have been titled *Refutations and Conjectures in Semantics and Syntax,* as one colleague has pointed out.

In addition to my associates in Holland, I was able to air some of this material with friends in Belgium, Egypt, England, and Scandinavia. Thanks go to Arnold Evers, Ger de Haan, Riny Huybregts, Jan Koster, and Henk van Riemsdijk for contributing to the discussion and keeping me honest during the course of the lectures, to Robert Bley-Vroman and Joel Hust for commenting on an earlier draft of the manuscript, to Joan Bresnan for criticizing excerpted portions of Part II, and most of all to Noam Chomsky, Joe Emonds, and Riny Huybregts for their detailed and thoughtful comments on the completed manuscript. I am grateful for the contributions and criticism of those involved and take this opportunity to emphasize that nobody has agreed with all of my exegesis, although some have disagreed with most. I owe a special debt of thanks to Henk Schultink, director of the linguistics institute in Utrecht, to Wobbina Kwast, director of the Netherlands-America Commission in Amsterdam, and to Luise Brame.

MICHAEL K. BRAME
University of Washington

Desist from thrusting out reasoning from your mind because of its disconcerting novelty. Weigh it, rather, with discerning judgment. Then, if it seems to you true, give in. If it is false, gird yourself to oppose it.

Lucretius

The Historical Setting

The descriptivist tradition dominated American linguistics throughout the fifties. This tradition, influenced by empiricist behaviorist doctrine, was preoccupied primarily with procedures for the segmentation and classification of linguistic data. Emphasis was placed on description to the almost total exclusion of explanation. Grammars were viewed as inventories or taxonomies of linguistic elements which were considered valid only if discovered by the aforementioned procedures. In this view, remarked Chomsky, "linguistics is thought of as a classificatory science." It is Chomsky's critique of the descriptivist tradition, of the behaviorist view of language, and of antimentalist attitudes that is responsible in large part for the almost complete abandonment of descriptive linguistics in the past decade or so. Chomsky's outlook has been justly considered by many to be revolutionary in character, and its impact on linguistics, psychology, and to a lesser extent, on philosophy and mathematics, bears witness to this interpretation.

What is most impressive about Chomsky's revolution is not so much his critique of the descriptive linguistics paradigm itself as the success his own approach to language enjoyed in providing explanations where others had provided mere descriptions. The later chapters of *Syntactic Structures* remain to this day a refreshing and fruitful source of explanations for many complex syntactic phenomena of English. Chomsky went on to raise questions which could not even be asked in the earlier framework. For example, he cited examples such as the following:

(1) a. Mary saw the boy walking towards the railroad station.
     b. What did Mary see the boy walking towards?
     c. Who(m) did Mary see walking towards the railroad station?
     d. Do you know the boy who(m) Mary saw walking towards the railroad station?
     e. The railroad station that Mary saw the boy walking towards is about to be demolished.

Chomsky noted that (1a) is ambiguous in the sense of being subject to interpretations analogous to the following:

(2) a. Mary saw the boy walk towards the railroad station.
     b. Mary saw the boy who was walking towards the railroad station.

The question Chomsky posed is this: Why are (1b–e) not ambiguous in the same way? In fact, (1b–e) elicit an interpretation related to (2a), not one analogous to (2b). His answer to this question has come to be known as the A-over-A principle, which was formulated as "a hypothetical linguistic universal." It required a certain degree of abstraction away from the actual strings displayed in (1); abstract sources of the relevant sentences were proposed and generated by phrase structure rules. A hierarchical or constituent structure was associated with each abstract sentence. Chomsky formulated transformational rules to relate the deep structures—the abstract sentences together with their constituent structures—to the surface structures. The motivation for these abstractions was precisely the fact that they served to shed light on questions such as that mentioned above. This refreshing generative approach to the study of language sparked the imagination of linguists and provided the most cogent reason for abandoning descriptive linguistics where the concept of generation was totally absent and where the structures actually treated, when made precise, are totally exhausted by phrase structure grammar to the total exclusion of transformations. Thus, Chomsky introduced into linguistics a theory sufficiently explicit to permit questions of adequacy to be raised for the first time. Confronted with an explicit theory, linguists gained a new source of questions; the theory could be applied to an ever-widening range of data and serious universal hypotheses could be ventured.

The work of the period between the publication of *Syntactic Structures* in 1957 and the publication of *Aspects of the Theory of Syntax* in 1965 was marked by several developments. During this period Chomsky and Halle had integrated transformational grammar with a phonological component, whose effect was to interpret surface structures, providing them with a phonetic representation. The impetus for much of this work, incidentally, can be traced back as far as 1951 to Chomsky's master's thesis [31]. Transformational grammar was also provided with a lexicon, recursion was moved from the transformational component to the phrase structure component or base, and the transformational cycle was introduced; meanwhile Katz and Fodor [79] attempted to integrate transformational grammar with a semantic component, although Fodor was soon to give up the enterprise as ill-conceived. A later refinement was the work of Katz and Postal [80], which was "a conception of the semantic component which claimed that projection rules are restricted to underlying P-markers" which expressed the "generalization that transformations do not affect meaning." Chomsky at first accepted the Katz-Postal hypothesis: "We are, in effect, assuming that the semantic interpretation of a sentence depends only on its lexical items and the grammatical functions and relations represented in the underlying structures in which they appear" [36: 136]. In a footnote to this remark, however, he insisted: "As it now stands, this claim seems to me somewhat too strong, though it is true in one important sense of semantic interpretation. . . . For example, it seems clear that the order of 'quantifiers' in surface structures sometimes plays a role in semantic interpretation." He continued, "Thus for many speakers—in particular, for me—the sentences 'everyone in the room knows at least two languages' and 'at least two languages are known by everyone in the room' are not synonymous." These examples had already been cited in *Syntactic Structures* [33: 100–101], and similar examples had been given by Chomsky as early as 1955, along with others, which, if valid, would refute the Katz-Postal hypothesis. Chomsky's 1955 observations are worth quoting at length:

> . . . it might be felt that such general relations between sentences as the active-passive relation have a semantic origin . . . Even the weakest semantic relation, that of factual equivalence, fails to hold in general between actives and their corresponding passives. This is most clearly the case for sentences containing the 'quantificational' words "all," "some," "several," numbers, etc. In order for "someone is liked by everybody" to be true, it is necessary that there be some single person whom everybody likes, while "everybody likes someone" may be true even if A and B have no common friends, as long as A likes C, B likes D, etc. Similarly, "several of them know every European language" may be false, but "every European language is known by several of them" true, if the group in question contains several native speakers from each European speech-community, but no one who knows every European language. Non-quantificational occurrences can also be found where one of an active-passive pair would normally be considered true, and the other false . . . If A has unwittingly and unintentionally done something which B took as an insult, it might be correct to say "B was insulted by A," but not "A insulted B." [32]

Chomsky's observations were echoed in Wang [157] some seven years later:

> . . . it is important to distinguish between using semantic labels heuristically . . . [and] using semantic criteria in the design of a grammar. The former, when used carefully, is not only helpful mnemonically, but also suggestive of correspondences that might or might not exist between the semantic and grammatical structures of the language. The latter usage, on the other hand, is harmful on two counts. One, we will have introduced criteria whose vagueness violates our desire for precision in our grammar. Secondly, since the semantic and grammatical structures are not isomorphic, these criteria will frequently lead us to wrong decisions. An example from English is the active-passive relation which has been mistakenly thought to be ''meaning-preserving.'' Had we taken this semantic criterion seriously, we would be disallowed from considering as being in an active-passive relation such sentences as
>
> a.   Everybody loves somebody.
> b.   Somebody is loved by everybody.
>
> which are clearly not equivalent semantically. [157: 192–193]

Chomsky proceeded to dismiss his own alleged counterexamples to the Katz-Postal hypothesis concerning deep structure and semantic interpretation on grounds similar to those adopted by Katz and Postal [80], and later by generative semanticists, and even went so far as to claim that the Katz-Fodor hypothesis ''is the basic idea that has motivated the theory of transformational grammar since its inception,'' an assertion which is difficult to reconcile with the work of *Syntactic Structures,* Klima's work on negation, and the early work on attachment transformations by Kuroda.[1] But shortly after accepting the Katz-Postal hypothesis, Chomsky changed his position to one consistent with his earlier counterexamples. We read, ''In fact, I think that a reasonable explication of the term 'semantic interpretation' would lead to the conclusion that surface structure also contributes in a restricted but important way to semantic interpretation . . .'' [37].

There emerged in the post-*Aspects* linguistic scene two views concerning linguistic semantics: 1) the older position, implicit in Chomsky's early work, and more explicit in the work of Kuroda, that both deep and surface structure are relevant to semantic interpretation, and 2) the Katz-Postal position, adopted momentarily, but with reservation by Chomsky, and apparently to this day by Katz. It was not long before a new linguistic school—generative semantics—whose leading exponents include Postal, Lakoff, Ross, and McCawley, laid claim to a second revolution in linguistics. Thus, Lakoff, in praise of a theoretical device of his theory, remarked, "This is as much an innovation over transformational grammar as transformational grammar is over phrase structure grammar" [91]. As noted above, phrase structure grammar exhausts the syntax of the descriptivist tradition. Lakoff's remark must be interpreted, therefore, as laying claim to a new revolution in linguistics of the stature of Chomsky's. In another work by Lakoff we read that the generative semantics results "have not been universally accepted, largely because the foundations of the field have been brought into question, in reaction, in part, to this work" [90]. Here Lakoff gives vent to a second boast for the revolutionary character of generative semantics.

Although Lakoff continues to be the most vocal of generative semanticists, it is Postal whose ideas have for the most part influenced and shaped the development of generative semantics. According to Lakoff, his 1965 treatise [86] is "an exploration into Postal's conception of grammar," and, according to Chomsky [38], it "incorporates many important suggestions by Paul Postal." In this work, Lakoff attempts to argue that adjectives are verbs, that adverbials of various types are really underlying predicates, that quantifiers are verbs, and so on.

Like Chomsky, who soon abandoned the Katz-Postal hypothesis concerning semantics, generative semanticists, including Postal, were also to deny its validity. But, whereas Chomsky and others argued for the feasibility of surface structure rules of interpretation, generative semanticists, to a large extent due to the influence of McCawley's writings, concluded that syntax and semantics should not be distinguished. Searle wrote,

> Those who call themselves generative semanticists believe that the generative component of a linguistic theory is not the syntax . . . but the semantics, that the grammar starts with a description of the meaning of a sentence and then generates the syntactical structures through the introduction of syntactical rules and lexical rules. The syntax then becomes just a collection of rules for expressing meaning. [148]

What began as a trend toward deeper underlying representations led to a concern for semantics, resulting in the rejection of any distinction between syntax and semantics. It is interesting to note in this connection that

Chomsky had foreseen such a development much earlier when he wrote, "as syntactic description becomes deeper, what appear to be semantic questions fall increasingly within its scope; and it is not entirely obvious whether or where one can draw a natural bound between grammar and 'logical grammar' . . . ." But he continued, "Nevertheless, it seems clear that explanatory adequacy for descriptive semantics requires, beyond this, the development of an independent semantic theory . . . that deals with questions of a kind that can scarcely be coherently formulated today . . ." [34: 936].

Lakoff's 1965 dissertation was eventually published as [90], and in the foreword to the latter, McCawley applauds the earlier dissertation [86] for casting "great light on the concept of 'grammatical category' by showing that the great profusion of category labels that had appeared in previous transformational work could be avoided and the inventory of categories reduced to a set that could lay some claim to universality."[2] This thirst for a reduction in the inventory of categories led McCawley in [107] to the "startling" conclusion that "tenses are not features but are themselves underlying verbs." It moved Ross [137] to argue that auxiliaries are, after all, main verbs. It inspired Carden [28] [29] to derive quantifiers from underlying verbs. Bach [5] chimed in with the claim that nouns derive from underlying predicates, and others followed suit with equally "astounding" results, such as that prepositions too are underlying predicates. And so forth.

The reduction of underlying grammatical categories is conveniently linked by generative semanticists to logic. McCawley claims that "symbolic logic, subject to certain modifications, provides an appropriate system for semantic representation within the framework of transformational grammar" [104]. The relationship between reduced categories and symbolic logic is clarified by McCawley in a revealing quote. A comment by Bresnan serves well to introduce it: "In what must be regarded as a *tour de force* of reductivism, McCawley chronicles how the syntactic categories fell one after another. . . ."[24]. McCawley wrote,

> Lakoff and Ross have argued in lectures at Harvard and MIT in Autumn 1966 that the only "deep" syntactic categories are *sentence, noun phrase, verb phrase, conjunction, noun,* and *verb,* and that all other traditionally recognized categories are special cases of these categories corresponding to the "triggering" of transformations by certain lexical terms. Bach [5] then discovered some quite convincing arguments that the *noun-verb* distinction need not be part of this

inventory of categories. . . . Lakoff observed that the resulting inventory of categories . . . matches in almost one-to-one fashion the categories of symbolic logic . . . if one accepts Fillmore's proposal that VP is not a "basic" category but a "derived" category . . . then not only is the correspondence between "deep" syntactic categories and the categories of symbolic logic exact, but the "phrase structure rules" governing the way in which the "deep" syntactic categories may be combined correspond exactly to the "formation rules" of symbolic logic . . . [106: 169]

Generative semantics, with its recourse to increasingly remote underlying structures, is thus seen to lead to Chomsky's 1962 observation that "as syntactic description becomes deeper, what appear to be semantic questions fall increasingly within its scope; and it is not entirely obvious whether or where one can draw a natural bound between grammar and 'logical grammar' . . ." Since Chomsky was prophetically aware of the possibility of such a development long before the generative semantics concert began, we must ask why he did not push generative semantics himself, and thus bring about the new revolution. My answer to this question is laid out in the following pages, which comprise Part I of these lectures.

NOTES

[1] Chomsky informs me that what he actually intended by the "basic idea" was the idea that underlying structural descriptions of sentences must support semantic interpretation.

[2] In this connection it should be noted that real strides are taken in the direction of universality with respect to base categories by Chomsky in [40], where rule schemata are introduced—i.e., bar notation. Chomsky's approach, however, does not involve the abolition of categories in deep structure.

Part I Generative Semantics

Chapter 1

Lexical Decomposition and the Growth of Syntactic Irregularity

. . . the main difference between Einstein and an amoeba . . . is that Einstein *consciously seeks for error elimination.* He tries to kill his theories: he is *consciously critical* of his theories which, for this reason, he tries to *formulate* sharply rather than vaguely. But the amoeba cannot be critical *vis-à-vis* its expectations or hypotheses: they are part of it.

Karl R. Popper

. . . there are fewer grammatical categories and grammatical relations in deep structure than had previously been thought . . . these are rather startling results and even more startling because they were arrived at without the statement of a single rule.

George Lakoff

The ultimate fate of any theory of language will be determined not so much by metatheoretical arguments for it as by its ability to deal with the bare primary data in a revealing and insightful manner, i.e., by its success in predicting systematic regularities in the data and in providing explanations for apparent irregularities. In order for any theory to be successful, it must at the very least offer an explicit characterization of the rules and formal devices proposed so as to provide a basis for comparison with competing theories. It is not enough to advance "bold" hypotheses and to list sixty-nine intuitive arguments for them; positive proposals must be accompanied by explicit formulations which can be tested and rejected in the face of the relevant evidence. Whereas phonologists and syntacticians have in the past been obliged to state their rules explicitly, generative semanticists have been free to wax theoretical in the absence of explicit formulations of the rules and formal devices employed. This development reverses the trend initiated by Chomsky in [32] and [33].

The search for rigorous formulation in linguistics has a much more serious motivation than mere concern for logical niceties or the desire to purify well-established methods of linguistic analysis. Precisely constructed models for linguistic structure can play an important role, both negative and positive, in the process of discovery itself. By pushing a precise but inadequate formulation to an unacceptable conclusion, we can often expose the exact source of this inadequacy and, consequently, gain a deeper understanding of the linguistic data. More positively, a formalized theory may automatically provide solutions for many problems other than those for which it was explicitly designed. [33: 5]

The point is almost too obvious to be discussed in print and yet the inexplicitness of generative semantics, which I will elaborate, is the key to its failure. This inexplicitness has served to camouflage certain conclusions which become obvious when the rules and assumptions of generative semantics are made explicit. The absence of explicit formulations is often justified with remarks such as the following:

In early studies linguists attempted to state precisely, using various symbols and notational conventions, the exact environmental conditions under which a particular rule applied. Unfortunately the notations were frequently cumbersome and showed much individual variation from author to author, so that the rules were hard to read. Partly in reaction to this overconcern with formalism and partly because of the feeling that it is premature, or even not possible, to write formal rules, later studies often merely state in ordinary language what rules are supposed to do. [132: ix]

This position contrasts sharply with Chomsky's early advice:

I think that some of those linguists who have questioned the value of precise and technical development of linguistic theory may have failed to recognize the productive potential in the method of rigorously stating a proposed theory and applying it strictly to linguistic material with no attempt to avoid unacceptable conclusions by ad hoc adjustment or loose formulation [33: 5]

Failure to heed this advice can lead to disastrous consequences. For example, Dougherty is speaking of generative semantics when he writes,

If a linguist does not formalize his description of some language phenomenon, it may well be that it cannot be formalized because: (a) There are internal contradictions among his underlying assumptions; and/or (b) The formal system delimited by the linguist's statements 'in ordinary language about what the rules are supposed to do' [132: ix] has little in common with the actual processes in language, i.e., the linguist's system may be incorrect (which would become obvious if it were formalized), or it may make no testable assertions about the structure of language. [52: 427]

Dougherty's remarks are borne out time and again when we consider analyses within the framework of generative semantics. To illustrate the dangers inherent in this cavalier method of inexplicitness, we may take as a fairly representative example, McCawley's "English as a VSO Language." As the title indicates, in this article McCawley claims that English has an underlying VSO (Verb–Subject–Object) order of constituents together with a post-cyclic transformation inverting the verb and subject to yield the surface SVO order of English. McCawley remarks that "an obvious question to ask, then, is what effect the assumption of underlying predicate-first order would have on the cycle in English." He concludes,

Of the 15 transformations of English that I can argue must be in the cycle, there are 10 for which it makes no significant difference whether they apply to structures with predicate first or predicate second. For the remaining five cyclic transformations, the underlying constituent order makes a significant difference in the complexity of the conditions under which the transformation applies, or in its effect. In each case, the version of the transformation that assumes predicate-first order is significantly simpler in the sense of either involving fewer elementary operations or applying under conditions which can be stated without the use of the more exotic notational devices that have figured in transformational rules. [105: 292]

In fact, had McCawley provided explicit rules and derivations consistent with the VSO hypothesis, he might have noticed that it entails a far more "exotic notational device" than any proposal within the standard theory adopting underlying SVO order. Thus, as noted by Berman in [11], cyclic Raising will apply to McCawley's underlying structure (1a) to give (1b).

(1)   a.   expect Joe [finish Mary her work] $\implies$ Raising
       b.   expect Joe Mary [finish her work]

But now post-cyclic Inversion will not only invert *expect* and *Joe* in the matrix clause of (1b), but also *finish* and *her work* in the embedded clause. This will lead to the ungrammatical result (2a), instead of the desired (2b).

(2)   a.   *Joe expected Mary her work to finish.
       b.   Joe expected Mary to finish her work.

Clearly, then, McCawley's post-cyclic inversion rule must incorporate an "exotic" device; it must not apply when Raising has "already" applied. As Berman has noted, within McCawley's framework, this post-cyclic rule must be formulated so as not to apply when other rules such as Equi-NP Deletion and still others have "already" applied. As so often happens when the underlying structures diverge in an unnatural way from the surface structures, as in the case of McCawley's underlying VSO, the abstraction raises more questions than it answers. Here the "global" formulation of the post-cyclic rule is simply an ad hoc consequence of the unnatural underlying order posited.[1]

The upshot of this discussion is simply this. Only when rules are explicitly formulated, and derivations provided, does the incorrectness of many of the "bold" hypotheses of generative semantics become obvious.

This conclusion has been arrived at by Schachter during the course of his careful critique of three generative semantics proposals for coalescing grammatical categories—[86], [139], and [5].

> To the extent . . . that Lakoff, Ross and Bach fail to prove their cases (and this extent is, I think, almost total), one may certainly feel free to reject their proposed coalescences of traditional categories . . . In addition to the substantive conclusion just stated, there is, I think, a methodological conclusion to which this critique also points: namely, that there is likely to be an inverse correlation between the amount of formal-rule writing a grammarian attempts and the likelihood that his arguments will fail on formal grounds. While *empirically* invalid arguments may be hard to avoid (since it is, alas, all too easy to overlook or misinterpret data), *formally* invalid arguments—i.e., invalid arguments concerning the generalizations that can and cannot be captured by different grammars—will, in most cases, automatically be avoided if these grammars are actually written . . . Now the three studies that have been the subject of this critique contain little or nothing in the way of formalization. (More specifically, Ross's paper contains little, the two others nothing, or next to nothing.) . . . The consequences of this choice are, I think, all too clear. [146: 186]

The generative semantics attitude is in marked contrast with what Chomsky had in mind when he wrote *Syntactic Structures*. It is also in marked contrast with the early Postal, who advocated explicitness on numerous occasions. For example, in criticizing Longacre's *Grammar Discovery Procedures*, the early Postal intoned,

> ... I would strongly suspect that the two most important 'discovery procedures' from the point of view of theoretical aims are neglected by Longacre. Namely, learn the language of study as well as possible and attempt to formulate an explicit account of the rules which generate the full syntactic structures of its sentences ... [122: 98]

And, when the early Postal inveighed against Martinet, he prophetically wrote of his later self when he said that "informality tends to conceal the inadequacies of any kind of description" [123]. One such description is generative semantics, as will be made clear in the following pages.

1.1 LEXICAL DECOMPOSITION

Generative semanticists "posit a great deal of transformational syntax inside, or behind, lexical items, especially verbs" [152: 5]. For example, according to generative semantics, the (b) examples of (3–6) derive from structures akin to the (a) examples.

(3) a. John struck Bill as being similar to a gorilla.
     b. Bill reminded John of a gorilla.

(4) a. The sauce came to be thick.
     b. The sauce thickened.

(5) a. John caused Harry to die.
     b. John killed Harry.

(6) a. Mary persuaded Bill not to go.
     b. Mary dissuaded Bill from going.

In all these examples, we see that simple words such as *remind, thicken, kill,* and *dissuade* are treated on a par with longer syntactic sequences. Generative semantics claims that well-motivated syntactic rules can be brought to bear in deriving them. Let us therefore investigate the arguments for such a claim.

1.1.1 *remind*

Postal has investigated the verb *remind* and concluded that "there is an elaborate array of evidence indicating that this element has a transformational derivation from a complex underlying source in which there is no single verbal element corresponding to *remind*" [124: 37]. Because no rules are explicitly given in this article, it is not clear that there is anything here to criticize. Still, I think that Postal's claim can be countered on the basis of any of the interpretations which may be given for the step-by-step development of his conclusions.

Postal's initial proposal for the underlying source of *remind* is provided in (7).

(7)   a.   me PERCEIVE [Larry SIMILAR Winston Churchill] $\implies$
     b.   Larry reminds me of Winston Churchill.

Postal remarks that such an analysis "of *remind* clauses claims that these should be paraphrases of sentences with *perceive* main verbs and complements involving assertions of similarity." Postal explicitly claims, then, that by adopting (7a) as the underlying structure of (7b), it follows that (7b) is a paraphrase of (8).

(8)   I perceive that Larry is similar to Winston Churchill.

Postal goes on to assert explicitly that this analysis also predicts that "just as [(9a)] is contradictory, so is [(9b)]."

(9)   a.   I perceive that Larry is similar to Winston Churchill although I perceive that Larry is not similar to Winston Churchill.
     b.   Larry reminds me of Winston Churchill although I perceive that Larry is not similar to Winston Churchill.

Postal concludes that these predictions are correct and that therefore they support the postulation of (7a) as the underlying representation of (7b). By what logic, we must ask, does the postulation of (7a) predict that (7b) is a paraphrase of (8) and that (9b) is contradictory because (9a) is contradictory? Postal offers no answer, but within this framework he must mean that (7a) is the underlying representation for both (7b) and (8). Since both (7b) and (8) have the same underlying representations, similar properties of

8

remind clauses and *perceive* clauses will be expected to emerge in surface structure.

Upon scrutiny we learn that Postal's predictions are false. Thus, Bowers [13] has shown that (9b) is not contradictory by citing examples such as the following:

(10)   For some reason Larry reminds me of Winston Churchill although I perceive that Larry is not really similar to him at all.

Sentence (10), unlike (9a), is not contradictory, indicating that the semantic properties of *remind* are not those intrinsic to *perceive as similar*. It is therefore dubious that (7b) and (8) derive from (7a) as suggested by Postal.

Postal goes on to argue that (11a) has many properties in common with (7b) and that both have a remote structure similar to (11b).

(11)   a.   Larry strikes me as being like Winston Churchill.
        b.   I strike [[Larry like Winston Churchill]$_S$]$_{NP}$

Now (7b) is derived from (11b) according to the following derivation in which a "poorly understood" rule of Psych Movement is conveniently summoned.

(12)   I strike [Larry like Winston Churchill] $\implies$ Raising
        I strike Larry [like Winston Churchill] $\implies$ Psych Movement
        Larry strike I like Winston Churchill $\implies$ *remind*-Formation
        Larry reminds me of Winston Churchill.

The derivation of *remind* sentences illustrated in (12) is referred to as the *strike-like* analysis. Presumably *remind*-Formation is intended here to be an optional rule. If it fails to apply, (11a) is the resulting sentence.

Already one senses that this analysis leaves much to be explained. For example, what is to ensure that an *as* is inserted to yield (11a) and that an *of* is inserted to yield (7b)? What guarantees that *being* is inserted to give (11a)? These facts are apparently considered to be trivial details, but in the absence of any explicit account, no such conclusion can be granted. Moreover, let us note that again Postal's analysis predicts that both of the following are contradictory:

(13)   a.   Larry strikes me as being like Winston Churchill although

Larry strikes me as not being like Winston Churchill.
b.   Larry reminds me of Winston Churchill although Larry strikes me as not being like Winston Churchill.

However, once again Bowers has shown this prediction to be false with an example similar to (14).

(14)   For some reason Larry reminds me of Winston Churchill although he strikes me (at the same time) as not being like him at all.

Given Postal's *strike-like* analysis of *remind,* one wonders why there should be a difference between the (a) and (b) examples of (15) and (16).[2]

(15)   a.   Every time he scratches, Harvey reminds me of my measles.
        b.   ? Every time he scratches, Harvey strikes me as being similar to my measles.

(16)   a.   When he slurps, Harvey reminds me of food.
        b.   ? When he slurps, Harvey strikes me as being similar to food.

Turning now to some of the arguments Postal adduces for the *strike-like* analysis, we encounter the following examples as evaluated by Postal:

(17)   a.   *Harry reminds himself of a gorilla.
        b.   *Harry reminds me of himself.
        c.   *Harry reminded me of myself.

According to Postal, the unacceptability of (17) is a consequence of the *strike-like* analysis. This follows from the abstract structure postulated by him. Thus, if (17a) and (17c) were in fact grammatical sentences of English, they would a fortiori constitute counterevidence to the *strike-like* analysis. As Kimball [82] has observed, (17a) and (17c) are in fact perfectly acceptable; Postal's incorrect judgments are simply a consequence of his failure to consider an appropriate context. Kimball clarifies the issue by providing such a context in terms of sentences such as the following:

(18)   a.   As Urman looked in the mirror, he suddenly reminded himself of a great overstuffed teddy bear.

b. Urchild is such a blunderer; she reminds me of myself sometimes.

Another argument Postal advances in support of the *strike-like* analysis of *remind* is the following: "the failure of *remind* to undergo Passive is derivable without special statement from the failure of *strike* to undergo this rule" [124: 58]. Thus, Postal adduces the following examples:

(19) a. *Harry was struck by a 1936 Chevrolet as being similar to a 1946 Packard.
b. *Harry was reminded of a 1936 Chevrolet by a 1946 Packard.

However, Ronat [133] notes that there are differences between *strike* and *remind* which should not be expected under the *strike-like* analysis.

(20) a. I was reminded of my youth by his actions.
b. *I was struck by his actions as being similar to my youth.

Additional counterexamples to Postal's *strike-like* analysis of *remind* will be adduced in chapter 3. Examples such as those provided by Bowers, Kimball, Ronat, and others firmly establish that Postal's abstract analysis cannot stand.

1.1.2 *thicken*

In [87] Lakoff has treated sentences such as the following:

(21) a. The sauce thickened.
b. The sauce became thick.
c. The sauce got thick.
d. The sauce turned thick.
e. The sauce grew thick.
f. The sauce came to be thick.

Lakoff comments: "We would like to suggest that the differences among these sentence types are all superficial, that the types are transformationally related, and that their underlying structures are essentially identical."

11

The putative identity of (21a–f), we are told, is based on identical underlying structures and similar derivations. Thus, the (21f) example is derived according to (22).

(22) it [for the sauce to be thick] came about $\Longrightarrow$ *it*-Replacement
      the sauce came about [for to be thick] $\Longrightarrow$ *about*-Deletion
      the sauce came [for to be thick] $\Longrightarrow$ *for*-Deletion
      the sauce came to be thick

We are told, "all of these transformational processes are independently motivated," but in fact some are highly conjectural. Lakoff claims, "we can derive 'the sauce became thick' and 'the sauce got thick' in essentially the same way if we consider 'become' and 'get' as verbs of the same class as 'come about', except that they undergo a further rule which deletes 'to be'." Elsewhere he remarks that " 'get', and 'grow' work essentially like 'become' when they function in change constructions," so 'the sauce became thick' would undergo a similar derivation. Thus,

(23) it [for the sauce to be thick] became $\Longrightarrow$ *it*-Replacement
      the sauce became [for to be thick] $\Longrightarrow$ *for*-Deletion
      the sauce became [to be thick] $\Longrightarrow$ *to be*-Deletion
      the sauce became thick

Similar derivations are proposed for (21c–e). And again these derivations are highly conjectural. For example, there is no evidence that *thick* should be represented as an S in underlying representations, nor is there evidence that *become* selects sentential subjects. Furthermore, no evidence to motivate *to be*-Deletion is adduced by Lakoff. Thus, besides the fact that none of these rules are explicitly formulated in Lakoff's article, they are not in fact independently motivated and must therefore be considered as no more than ad hoc. In this connection, it should be pointed out that Lakoff has evidently misunderstood what would constitute independent motivation. Lakoff has taken Rosenbaum's arguments for the existence of *it*-Replacement [135] as the independent evidence in support of his derivations. However, even assuming that Rosenbaum is justified in positing *it*-Replacement for his examples, it does not follow that the rule should be utilized for examples that diverge rather drastically in surface structure. By reasoning similar to Lakoff's, we could conclude that *big* in *it is big* derives from a sentential source in subject position, etc. Clearly, such reasoning is unacceptable and can only lead to absurdities.

We are now left with (21a), which, according to Lakoff, "would have the same deep structure except that instead of containing a real verb, it would contain the bundle of grammatical features that define the class of 'come about', 'become', 'get', etc., and that together carry the meaning common to the items in the class." The resulting derivation is the following:

(24)   it [for the sauce to be thick] CHANGE $\Longrightarrow$ *it*-Replacement
    the sauce CHANGE [for to be thick] $\Longrightarrow$ *for*-Deletion
    the sauce CHANGE [to be thick] $\Longrightarrow$ *to be*-Deletion
    the sauce CHANGE thick $\Longrightarrow$ CHANGE-Substitution
    the sauce thick $\Longrightarrow$ *en*-Affixation
    the sauce thickened

In this derivation CHANGE is the abstract verb carrying "the meaning common to the items in the class." It is significant that Lakoff nowhere tells us what that meaning is. He claims to account for semantic paraphrase relations, but is unable to do so explicitly. Moreover, although Lakoff claims that the "single new rule" in the derivation is the putative rule of CHANGE-Substitution, there is actually a second "new rule": "The appropriate ending, in this case '-en', would be added on by a later affixation rule to all adjectives that underwent the rule VERB OF CHANGE SUBSTITUTION." The ad hoc nature of this rule will become clear directly.

Lakoff's conclusion is the following: "by the addition to the grammar of English of one rule, we are able to relate verbs of change to their paraphrases." In other words, *become, get, turn, grow, come about,* and CHANGE are predicates of English forming a natural class and the putative paraphrase relations of (21a–f) are expressed by means of similar derivations, i.e., (22–24), which require "the addition to the grammar of English of one rule." This result is considered by generative semanticists to be of great moment, for, on the one hand, paraphrase relations are expressed and, on the other, it appears that English underlying structures are far more abstract "than hitherto suspected." There lingers some doubt in the minds of more critical-minded linguists.

In the first place, not one, but a host of special rules is required. In (24), for example, the unmotivated rules of CHANGE-Substitution and *en*-Affixation are required. But consider the following examples:

(25) a. The iron liquefied.
      b. The bomb deactivated.

Derivations analogous to (24) for these examples would require additional ad hoc rules, one to affix -*fy* and one to affix -*ate*.

In the second place, the rule of *to be*-Deletion requires further ad hoc theoretical elaboration in view of the fact that it must not apply to (21f) and yet must apply to (21b) and (21d).

(26) a. *The sauce came thick.
      b. *The sauce became to be thick.
      c. *The sauce turned to be thick.

Thus, Lakoff must somehow ensure that *to be*-Deletion will apply obligatorily to avoid (26b, c) and that it will not apply at all so as to avoid (26a). But the rule must be made optional so as to account for (27) beside (21e).

(27) The sauce grew to be thick.

Hence, *to be*-Deletion must be made optional for *grow*, obligatory for *become* and *turn*, and must be blocked for *come (about)*. These observations make it highly unlikely that *to be*-Deletion expresses any "generalization" in any reasonable sense of this term. Whether or not there is an instance of *to be* following the appropriate predicate should not be a property of *to be*-Deletion but rather a property of the lexical item in question. Within Chomsky's framework [36], such idiosyncratic properties are so expressed. But this all suggests that *to be*-Deletion is not a rule at all so that all of Lakoff's derivations must be rejected in view of the fact that they make crucial use of it.

In a similar vein, the rule of *en*-Affixation is equally suspect. Why, we must ask, does *thick* undergo *en*-Affixation after substitution for CHANGE in (24), but not *liquid*, which must undergo *fy*-Affixation, and vice versa? Within Lakoff's framework, special features or devices must be invented to "trigger" the appropriate rules. But this just shows that *en*-Affixation, *fy*-Affixation, *ate*-Affixation, etc., are really reflections of idiosyncratic lexical properties, which the standard theory captures in a straightforward way by taking the suffixes to be part of the lexical representations themselves. Lakoff's analysis is no more than a tortuous description of these uninteresting facts.[3]

The problem is even compounded within the generative semantics framework, since there are forms that undergo none of Lakoff's affixation rules. For example,

(28)   The liquid cooled.

And there are others which must undergo a deaffixation rule:

(29)   a.   The window broke.
        b.   The window is broken.

Here the adjective underlying (29a) is, according to Lakoff, *broken,* with affix *-en,* and yet the verb of change does not exhibit *-en* as a result of CHANGE-Substitution. Therefore Lakoff must provide a rule of deaffixation and ensure that it does not apply to examples such as *thicken,* or else further complicate CHANGE-Substitution. Lakoff fails to provide any rules to generate any of these data and is apparently unaware of the problems involved. These examples once again illustrate the danger inherent in vague, inexplicit work.

It would not be difficult to multiply the arguments against Lakoff's approach to verbs of change. However, I will content myself here with one last fact. Alongside Lakoff's paradigm with *cool,* one encounters a similar paradigm with *warm.*

(30)   a.   The liquid became $\left\{ \begin{matrix} cool \\ warm \end{matrix} \right\}$.

        b.   The liquid got $\left\{ \begin{matrix} cool \\ warm \end{matrix} \right\}$.

        c.   The liquid grew $\left\{ \begin{matrix} cool \\ warm \end{matrix} \right\}$.

        d.   The liquid came to be $\left\{ \begin{matrix} cool \\ warm \end{matrix} \right\}$.

Now, recall that these examples will all have similar derivations. We must then ask why *warm* cannot, although *cool* must, undergo CHANGE-Substitution, as illustrated in (31).

(31)   a.   The liquid cooled.
        b.   *The liquid warmed.

What these examples show is that Lakoff's analysis raises some insuperable difficulties, for it must somehow exclude the insertion of *warm* into a structure such as (32).

(32)   It [for the liquid to be warm] CHANGE

Since *the liquid is warm* is grammatical, it is not obvious that Lakoff will be able to overcome the difficulty raised by (31b). Within the standard theory the distinction is trivial. Items such as *cool* are specified lexically as both a verb and an adjective, but *warm* is marked as an adjective only. However, since *cool* as a verb of change is derived from an adjective in Lakoff's framework, the new problem of excluding (32) while allowing an identical structure with *cool* substituted for *warm* becomes crucial. Apparently, Lakoff would prevail upon some new device, such as his exception features [90], to exclude (32). The feature would require *warm* not to meet the structural description of CHANGE-Substitution. However, this ad hoc device is simply another name for the nonverbal nature of *warm* which is expressed directly in the standard theory. Moreover, it leads to a further loss of generalization, for what is to block the following as *underlying* structures in Lakoff's theory?

(33)   a.   *The room warmed.
       b.   *John thinks that the room warmed.

Clearly, (33a, b) are ungrammatical because *warm* is not a verb (as opposed to, say, *warm up*), and this fact must be expressed in Lakoff's framework to prohibit (33) as underlying structures. As a consequence of CHANGE-Substitution, however, the same facts are duplicated; (33a, b) are ruled out as deep structures (and hence as surface structures) because *warm* is not a verb, whereas (31b) is ruled out as a derived structure, made possible by CHANGE-Substitution, by some ad hoc exception feature. Again, the abstractions raise more problems than they solve and lead to a loss of generalization. Such obvious arguments suggest rather strongly that abstract predicates such as CHANGE do not exist.

It should be obvious from the foregoing discussion that many of the facts discussed by Lakoff should be treated as idiosyncratic lexical facts and, following Chomsky [36], expressed as contextual features of individual lexical items. Such an approach, as opposed to Lakoff's, affords us some hope of constraining the power of transformations, which appears to me to

16

be the underlying motivation for dealing with irregularity in the lexicon. We might even go so far as to prohibit lexical exceptions to syntactic rules by banning features of the type $[-\text{Rule } n]$ from the lexicon altogether.

1.1.3 *kill*

An abstract source for a class of causatives is also proposed in [87]. Lakoff there considers the following to be paraphrases, and the putative paraphrase relations are allegedly expressed by again adopting similar derivations:

(34) a. John thickened the sauce.
      b. John brought it about that the sauce thickened.
      c. John caused the sauce to thicken.
      d. John made the sauce thicken.

These examples will all have similar underlying representations:

(35) a. John CAUSE it [for it
          [for the sauce to be thick] to CHANGE]

      b. John brought about it [for it
          [for the sauce to be thick] to CHANGE]

      c. John caused it [for it
          [for the sauce to be thick] to CHANGE]

      d. John made it [for it
          [for the sauce to be thick] to CHANGE]

Thus, Lakoff claims that (34a–d) all undergo the CHANGE-Substitution transformation. In view of the discussion of the previous subsection, however, none of Lakoff's analyses can stand. Moreover there is little motivation for many of the putative rules Lakoff draws on. Consider, for example, the derivation of (34a) from (35a).

(36)   [John CAUSE it [for it [for the sauce to be thick]$_{S_1}$ to
                            CHANGE]$_{S_2}$]$_{S_3}$ $\Longrightarrow$ *it*-Replacement

          S_2 – CYCLE:

          for the sauce to CHANGE for to be thick $\Longrightarrow$ *for*-Deletion

17

for the sauce to CHANGE to be thick $\implies$ *to be-* Deletion
for the sauce to CHANGE thick $\implies$ CHANGE-Substitution
for the sauce to thick $\implies$ *en-* Affixation
for the sauce to thicken
S_3 — CYCLE:

John CAUSE it [for the sauce to thicken] $\implies$ *it-* Replacement
John CAUSE the sauce for to thicken $\implies$ *for-* Deletion
John CAUSE the sauce to thicken $\implies$ *to-* Deletion
John CAUSE the sauce thicken $\implies$ CAUSE-Substitution
John thicken the sauce.

Here we see that Lakoff has invented a new abstract predicate CAUSE in order to force (34a) into a pattern more like (34b–d). Now it is obvious that, with a little effort, we could force every sentence of the English language into any pattern desired with the artifice of abstract predicates. Moreover, the abstract predicate CHANGE has already been dismissed in section 1.1.2 above. There is, in addition, an inconsistency in Lakoff's description of the rules giving rise to (36). He remarks that (34a) is generated "after the deletion of 'for–to' by the same rule that applies to 'make' sentences . . ." There is apparently an attempt here to make (36) appear more plausible by calling two rules—*for-* Deletion and *to-* Deletion—one rule, *for–to–* Deletion. This, however, is inconsistent with his earlier remark on the derivation of (34d) from (35d): " . . . *make* . . . unlike 'cause' . . . undergoes a subsequent rule which deletes 'to'." Thus, Lakoff requires a special ad hoc rule of *to-* Deletion. But how is it guaranteed that *to-* Deletion will apply to *make* and CAUSE to yield (34d) and (34a), but not to *cause* to yield the ungrammatical **John caused the sauce thicken?* Again, an ad hoc feature must be invoked and this device again indicates that the distributional possibilities are most appropriately expressed in the lexicon as in the standard theory, not as an ad hoc fact about *to-* Deletion. In other words, *to-* Deletion does not exist. It would not be difficult to provide a battery of arguments against Lakoff's analysis of (34), but there seems to be little point in protracting the discussion. Therefore, it will be of some interest to turn to a second analysis of causatives, this one proposed by McCawley and enthusiastically endorsed by the generative semantics camp.

McCawley's analysis is based, in part, on his VSO analysis, which, as noted at the beginning of this chapter, has been refuted by Berman [11]. In view of this refutation, the analysis collapses, but for the sake of argument, let us investigate it here.

McCawley discusses the lexical item *kill* and claims that it derives from a source closer to *cause x to become not alive*. His derivation is repeated below.

(37) [CAUSE x [BECOME [NOT [ALIVE y]$_S$]$_S$]$_S$]$_S$ $\Longrightarrow$ Predicate-Raising
[CAUSE x [BECOME [NOT ALIVE] y]$_S$]$_S$]$_S$ $\Longrightarrow$ Predicate-Raising
[CAUSE x [BECOME NOT ALIVE] y]$_S$]$_S$ $\Longrightarrow$ Predicate-Raising
[CAUSE BECOME NOT ALIVE] x y]$_S$ $\Longrightarrow$ Lexical Insertion
[kill x y]

The capitalized items are McCawley's "semantic predicates" which must be distinguished from his "lexical items" which result from his rules of lexical insertion, in this case, CAUSE BECOME NOT ALIVE $\Longrightarrow$ *kill*. The post-cyclic rule of Subject-Inversion (which Berman has refuted) yields the sentence x *killed* y. Thus, by the artifice of Predicate-Raising in English, for which absolutely no syntactic evidence is offered, McCawley claims to have related pairs such as the following:

(38) a. John killed Harry.
       b. John caused Harry to die.

He writes that Predicate-Raising is "optional, since there is no need to perform all stages of the last derivation." He continues: "For example, by failing to perform the last application of predicate-raising, one would obtain sentences such as *John caused Harry to die.*" In deriving the latter, McCawley invokes his lexical insertion rule BECOME NOT ALIVE $\Longrightarrow$ *die* and CAUSE $\Longrightarrow$ *cause*.

There are numerous apparent difficulties with McCawley's analysis. There is first the difficulty of making the rules explicit, which is a perennial attribute of such work. Second, since Predicate-Raising is optional, and certainly rules such as ALIVE $\Longrightarrow$ *alive,* etc., are part of McCawley's theory, what is to prevent the following from being generated?

(39) *John caused Harry to become $\left\{ \begin{matrix} \text{not alive} \\ \text{dead} \end{matrix} \right\}$.

McCawley's approach predicts that (39) are well-formed sentences, but they are not. Therefore his analysis fails to attain the lowest level of adequacy, that of observational adequacy. Moreover, the underlying representations of (38a) and (38b) are identical within McCawley's framework, and it is therefore somewhat egregious not to recognize that *John killed Harry* and *John caused Harry to die* are not synonymous. This had already been pointed out almost a decade earlier in [67]. Thus, Hall noted the following contrasts (cf. also [112]):

(40) a.   A change in molecular structure caused the window to break.
      b.   *A change in molecular structure broke the window.

(41) a.   The low air pressure caused the water to boil.
      b.   *The low air pressure boiled the water.

(42) a.   The angle at which the door was mounted caused it to open whenever it wasn't latched.
      b.   *The angle at which the door was mounted opened it whenever it wasn't latched.

Davidson in [49] had made similar observations by citing the following:

(43) a.   The doctor removed the patient's appendix.
      b.   The doctor brought it about that the patient has no appendix.

Davidson observed, "The doctor may bring it about that the patient has no appendix by turning the patient over to another doctor who performs the operation; or by running the patient down with his Lincoln Continental. . . . In neither case would we say the doctor removed the patient's appendix."

More recently Chomsky has echoed these remarks by pointing to examples such as the following (cf. [41: fn. 15]):

(44) a.   John's clumsiness caused the door to open (the window to break).
      b.   *John's clumsiness opened the door (broke the window).

Elsewhere Chomsky has remarked,

> . . . John's negligence can cause the toast to burn, but it cannot burn the toast. Similarly, I can cause someone to die by arranging for him to

20

drive cross-country with a pathological murderer, but I could not properly be said to have killed him, in this case. [42: fn. 7]

Finally, in [61] Fodor has advanced considerable evidence to refute the generative semantics approach to causatives. Two of his examples which bring the relevant differences clearly into relief are repeated in (45) and (46).

(45) a.   John caused Mary to die and it surprised me that she did so.
      b.   *John killed Mary and it surprised me that she did so.

(46) a.   John caused Bill to die on Sunday by stabbing him on Saturday.
      b.   *John killed Bill on Sunday by stabbing him on Saturday.

Under the generative semantics approach of McCawley and others, one should not expect to find the pronounced differences between the pairs discussed by so many authors.[4] Under the standard theoretical approach, such differences are to be expected because the pairs cited above derive from different deep structures. Causatives, then, provide a cogent argument against generative semantics.

There have been attempts to save the generative semantics analysis of *kill* in the face of examples such as (45) and (46) adduced by Fodor. First, Lakoff and Ross have proposed the following condition to counter (45):

(47) If the lexical item and the antecedent are not morphologically related, the sentence is unacceptable. [95: 122]

Since *die* and *kill* are morphologically unrelated, Lakoff and Ross claim that principle (47) accounts for the ungrammaticality of (45b), while allowing for (45a). However, Smith [154] claims that the Lakoff-Ross principle makes false predictions. Thus, Smith considers (48) to be fully acceptable.

(48) The cyanide finally killed Boris, but it would have taken arsenic much longer to bring it about.

A second defense of the generative semantics analysis of *kill* is proposed by Seuren [152]. Seuren claims that examples analogous to (45a) are as ungrammatical as (45b), but this is clearly false and is perhaps due to the fact that he is not a native speaker of English. Even Lakoff and Ross in [95] accept Fodor's distinction. As for the difference between (46a) and (46b), Seuren attempts to provide for this distinction by resort to further unacceptable theoretical elaborations. He is forced to the unacceptable position that *by stabbing him on Saturday* and *on Sunday* are underlying "higher predicates" and that the underlying representation for (46a) is (49).

(49)   [by stabbing him on Saturday [cause John
       [on Sunday [die Bill]$_S$]$_S$]$_S$

True to the generative semantics tradition, Seuren fails to formulate rules for lowering and positioning of the adverbs and to provide evidence that these adverbs are underlying predicates. He also fails to note that there are arguments in the literature against such a position (cf. [43], [74]).

Seuren's point, however, is that the "predicate" *on Sunday* "prevents the unification of 'cause to die' into one item *kill.*" Seuren then proceeds to refute his own suggestion while simultaneously failing to apprehend as much when he observes, "If we adopt this explanation [sic], however, the question arises why *almost,* which must be considered an operator [predicate] too in terms of semantic syntax [generative semantics], should be allowed to modify embedded sub-lexical verbs freely enough to give rise to the ambiguity" noted earlier. In other words, *almost* is also a predicate within the generative semantics framework, but when it intervenes in place of *on Sunday* in (49), Predicate-Raising is not blocked. Now to overcome the new problem, Seuren introduces the deus ex machina:

> Without going into these problems too deeply here, we might suggest that a possible answer could be found in a distinction between referring and non-referring expressions. We speak of referring expression when it maps on to an element in a universe of interpretation. (Such elements may correspond to what, in a reasonably sound ontology, we take to be entities in the world, but may also be the product of 'internal' cognitive processes: fictional characters, or elements such as 'the average age of Londoners'.) [152: 12]

In view of his failure to provide an explicit account of the "possible answer," Seuren's proposal will not be discussed further.

1.1.4 *dissuade*

As a final illustration of lexical decomposition in generative semantics, consider Lakoff's analysis of *dissuade* set forth in [89] and [92]. According to Lakoff, "dissuade means *persuade*-NP-not" [89: 134] so that (50a) and (50b) have identical underlying representations.

(50) a. Mary persuaded Bill not to go.
      b. Mary dissuaded Bill from going.

However, (50a) and (50b) are not synonymous, as Chomsky has noted, since *dissuade,* but not *persuade not,* "presupposes some sort of intention on the part of the person dissuaded" [43: 143]. Thus, (50b) is appropriate only if Bill intended to go, but (50a) would be appropriate even if Bill had not made up his mind. Furthermore, the striking syntactic similarity between *persuade*-not and *persuade* versus the striking dissimilarity between *dissuade* and *persuade* is completely accidental within Lakoff's analysis, as pointed out by Hust in an excellent discussion of these constructions. Thus, Hust [71] notes the following similarities and differences:

(51) a. I persuaded him (not) to come.
      b. *I dissuaded him to come.

(52) a. I persuaded him that he should (not) come.
      b. *I dissuaded him that he should come.

(53) a. *I persuaded him from (not) coming.
      b. I dissuaded him from coming.

Such facts as these again support the standard theory, since *persuade* and *dissuade* are separate lexical items and therefore may bear different subcategorial restrictions; likewise, *persuade* and *persuade not* should exhibit similar co-occurrence restrictions. By contrast, within the theory of generative semantics, one expects to find a high degree of similarity between *persuade-not* and *dissuade,* but the facts do not bear out this prediction.

1.2   THE GROWTH OF SYNTACTIC IRREGULARITY
IN GENERATIVE SEMANTICS

In a recent critique of generative semantics, Bresnan has written the following:

> It should not be surprising that the use of rule features implies the absence of syntactic generalizations—they were devised, after all, to describe exceptions and irregularity. What is surprising is that rule features are used systematically by those who claim to have dispensed with deep structure: deep structure has been eliminated at the cost of making syntax systematically irregular. [24]

Another way of making the point is this: Deep structure is essentially the locus of distributional irregularity in the standard theory. If irregularity is spread over the transformational component, as in generative semantics, we lose all hope of constraining the power of transformations. If, on the other hand, as a working hypothesis, we account for irregularity prior to the application of transformational rules, then the future for the notion "transformation" looms much brighter.

Now the analyses discussed in section 1.1 are examples supplementing and supporting Bresnan's interpretation of generative semantics as a move toward syntactic irregularity. Thus, in the section on *thicken,* it was noted that putative rules such as *to be*-Deletion, *to*-Deletion, *en*-Affixation, *fy*-Affixation, etc., must be formulated with special features so that some lexical items, but not others, could be coded so as to undergo them. The point was made repeatedly that the distributional facts should be expressed in the lexicon, which is what is done in the standard theory. Thus, the fact that *become thick* is well-formed, while *come thick* is not, should not be expressed as a fact about irregularity, where *come to be thick* is "marked" as an exception to *to be*-Deletion, and *become to be thick* is not. Rather, *become* should be lexically subcategorized to select an adjective and *come* to select a verb phrase (VP). Thus, the fact that there is no *become to be thick* is comparable to the fact that there is no *pinch to be thick;* the fact that *become thick* is possible is comparable to the fact that *be thick* is possible. Both *become* and *be* select adjectives. Neither *become* nor *whisper* select VP complements, etc. Thus, it is simply not accurate to respond that subcategorization features are as arbitrary as the irregularity devices of generative semantics in terms of exception features and ad hoc transformations. For, it will not do to derive *become thick* from *become to be thick* by *to be*-Deletion for obvious reasons.

Therefore, the growth of syntactic irregularity in generative semantics is a consequence of more abstract analyses, elimination of deep structure, and proliferation of ad hoc transformations and exception features and devices; so it is here in conjunction with section 1.1 that we see a good reason for dismissing generative semantics as a serious theory of language. Generative semantics is a theory of ''systematic irregularity,'' whereas what is wanted is a theory of language.

Lexical decomposition is simply a special case of this systematic irregularity, for there are abundant examples from generative semantics which do not involve lexical decomposition per se and yet still lead to the same odious consequences. Bresnan's critique is given over to one such case [24].

In section 1.1 we have seen that there is no evidence for lexical decomposition based on some of the central examples advanced in its support. This leads one to conjecture that lexical decomposition is not a property of natural language and that the theory of language should prohibit it. In this connection, let us return to the discussion of causatives and to Fodor's conclusion:

> . . . even where a phrase and a word are synonymous, the former will characteristically exhibit degrees of syntactic freedom unavailable to the latter . . . There is thus a dilemma. Either *lexicalization* carries these unwanted degrees of freedom over into surface structure, thereby predicting sentences which are in fact ungrammatical, or special, ad hoc constraints have to be instituted to insure that *lexicalization* does not apply to phrases in which these degrees of freedom have been exploited. This seems to me to be a principled reason for doubting that there are transformations which map phrases onto words. [61: 437]

It is to the credit of the standard theory of transformational grammar that it does prohibit lexical decomposition. This prohibition is a consequence of deep structure, to which we turn in the next chapter.

We see in summary that generative semantics with its transformational excesses and abstract underlying structures serves as a breeding ground for irregularity. As syntax becomes more abstract,[5] transformations become more irregular, until ultimately the point is reached where the concept of transformation loses all content. An explicit formulation of the transformations in question would, of course, have revealed the misdirection of the generative semantics program in the first place. It is at this point that we begin to understand the change of face of those who once advocated explicitness and ridiculed vagueness.

NOTES TO CHAPTER 1

[1]When I impute abstractness to generative semantics throughout the following discussion, I will be using the term in a narrow sense. In general, more "transformations" apply to underlying representations to yield surface structures within the framework of generative semantics than do in the standard theory. In another, important sense, generative semanticists must be characterized as antiabstractionists, as noted by Ronat [133], Dougherty [53], and Katz and Bever [78] who argue that generative semantics represents a return to the canons of descriptivism and narrow empiricism. Chomsky puts it succinctly as follows:

> I think the point is that they [generative semanticists] are unwilling to stray far, in abstractness, from "the given"—i.e., phonetic fact and semantic fact. Structures that do not directly mirror one or the other are unacceptable. Hence, the virtual demise of syntax.
> (Chomsky, personal communication, 13 August 1975)

This antiabstractionist character of generative semantics is embodied in Lakoff's "natural logic" and "external motivation" and is largely responsible for his refusal to consider abstractions and generalizations expressed by phrase structure rules, certain syntactic categories, etc. For example, Lakoff [93: 86] criticizes an analysis of comparatives in [8] as "strange" because "it uses categories AP and DEG, which as usual have no external motivation."

In still another more radical sense generative semanticists are antiabstractionists. More recently, for example, Lakoff has defined generative semantics as the theory that incorporates grammar, semantics, situation, intention, mood, etc., and others, like Ross, have incorporated perceptual factors, belief, etc. (In other words, anything goes.) Within generative semantics, as it is most currently conceived, every fact is on a par with others; thus, no abstractions are permitted. This attitude does indeed represent a return to the canons of narrow empiricism.

[2]In [133], Ronat considers the possibility of adopting a *make-think* analysis of *remind* in place of Postal's *strike-like* analysis. She proceeds to argue against such an analysis, citing numerous differences such as the following:

(i)   a.   This song makes me think of the sonata I hope to compose.

        b.   This song reminds me of the sonata I hope to compose.

(ii)   a.   This child makes her think of the baby she's expecting.

        b.   This child reminds her of the baby she's expecting.

Indeed the (b) examples appear to be semantically peculiar, whereas there is nothing strange about the (a) examples. Ronat [133] also provides additional arguments against the *strike-like* analysis of *remind*.

[3]Bresnan has argued in [19] that word stress in English is assigned in the lexicon, or at least pretransformationally. Thus, it follows that stress-affecting suffixes such as *-ate, -fy,* etc., must be part of lexical entries. Thus, Bresnan's results, if correct, constitute further evidence disconfirming Lakoff's analysis.

[4]Additional criticism of the generative semantics analysis of *kill* can be found in Chomsky [43], Cruse [47], Ruwet [144: chap. 4], and chapter 3 below.

[5]See note 1 for a clarification of "abstractness in generative semantics."

Chapter 2

Deep Structure vs. Natural Logic

. . . symbolic logic, subject to certain modifications, provides an appropriate system for semantic representation within the framework of transformational grammar. I thus hold that the much-criticized title, *The Laws of Thought,* which George Boole (1840) gave to the first work on symbolic logic, is actually much more appropriate than has generally been thought the case.

James D. McCawley

Boole, in a work which he called the *Laws of Thought* . . . was also mistaken in supposing that he was dealing with the laws of thought. . . . His book was in fact concerned with formal logic. . . .

Bertrand Russell

. . . the formal properties of surface structures cannot diverge too greatly from those of deep structures without destroying the relationship between syntax and prosodic stress. In a sense, it is natural that a close relationship should exist between sound and syntactic structure; after all, languages, unlike the countless logics and "logical languages" invented by philosophers, are spoken. It is not surprising that McCawley's system, explicitly modeled on one kind of notation used in symbolic logic, proves to be an inadequate syntactic basis for a description of English stress contours.

Joan W. Bresnan

2.1 GENERATIVE SEMANTICS AS A SOURCE OF EVIDENCE FOR DEEP STRUCTURE

It is well known that generative semanticists chalk up the elimination of deep structure as one of their "results." It is not so well known that all of their arguments against deep structure can be turned against them. The concept of deep structure, introduced in [36], plays a major role in the standard theory. Deep structures are the most abstract syntactic structures. The level of deep structure is the level at which lexical items are inserted from the lexicon into the abstract structures generated by the phrase structure rules. It is the level which serves as input to the first transformational rule. Since all lexical items must be inserted before the transformational rules commence to operate, it follows that there can be no "syntax inside, or behind, lexical items," as generative semanticists would have it [152: 5]. In other words, there can be no lexical decomposition in the sense discussed in the previous chapter. But this, in view of the discussion of chapter 1, is, after all, a highly desirable consequence. That the standard theory should already prohibit analyses that can be refuted on internal grounds certainly speaks for its ability to correctly predict what constitutes human language, at least insofar as it is counterposed to generative semantics. This of course is Bresnan's point when she remarks that "deep structure has been eliminated at the cost of making syntax systematically irregular" [24].

To drive home the point, let us return to Postal's *strike-like* analysis of *remind*. Postal himself elucidates the point and brings it sharply into focus when he remarks,

> . . . [the generative semantics] analysis of *remind* clauses is simply incompatible with the Classical Theory of transformational grammar. In particular, it is incompatible with its assumption that there is a level of Deep Structure which is *distinct from* the level of Semantic Representation and which contains in it structures corresponding directly to the lexical items of the Surface Structure. [124: 99–100]

Notice that there are strong empirical reasons (discussed in section 1.1) for concluding that Postal's *strike-like* analysis is false. Now we have it by Postal's own admission that the standard theory, in particular *deep structure,* rules out the strike-like analysis of *remind* as a possible analysis consistent with the primary data of a natural language. But this, then, is a most desirable result. By incorporating a level of deep structure, the standard theory automatically eliminates much of the lexical prestidigitation we have observed to be characteristic method of generative semantics; therefore, the standard theory must be favored.

A similar point can be made with regard to the other examples discussed in the preceding chapter. For example, the standard theory, in view of deep structure, is simply incompatible with McCawley's claim that *kill* derives from the abstract structures he claims underlie *cause to become not alive.*

And, again, this is a desirable result in view of the fact that it predicts that *kill* and *cause to die* are not synonymous.

In this connection it should be noted that generative semantics does not stop with *kill*. It postulates abstract causatives for much else, and, like the uncritical amoeba of Popper, fails to confront the substantial counterevidence. Here we may turn to the interesting study of Cruse [47], who provides a generative semantics formulation for a number of putative causatives, including *teach,* and writes, ''they [the generative semantics formulations] fail to formalize our intuition that the various meanings belong naturally together.'' He concludes, ''It is difficult to avoid the conclusion that *teach* must occur as an element of deep structure.''

2.2   APPARENT ARGUMENTS CONTRA DEEP STRUCTURE

In the generative semantics literature there can be found several apparent arguments against deep structure. Here I would like to discuss two of those arguments and to show that, contrary to the claims voiced, the data discussed actually support the standard theory.

2.2.1   POSTAL ON PORK

It is remarkable, and also ironic, that Postal asserts that ''notably, no justification for the extra apparatus [deep structure] of Classical Theory *vis-à-vis* Generative Semantics is known . . .'' [124: 111]. This assertion is remarkable in view of the fact that Chomsky's papers [40] and [41] are given over in large part to a justification of deep structure. It is ironic in view of the fact that Postal's *strike-like* analysis provides additional justification for deep structure, as argued above.

In fact, Postal provides further evidence for deep structure, even though he is unaware of doing so. For, in his *remind* paper, he cites the following examples and asserts that the ''key fact . . . is that it [(1b)] is an essential paraphrase of [(1a)].''

(1)   a.   Harry likes meat from pigs.
      b.   Harry likes pork.

This ''key fact'' is explained, according to Postal, by generative semantics since (1b) derives from (2) by rules reducing relative clauses, etc.

31

(2) Harry likes meat which $\left\{ {\text{is} \atop \text{comes}} \right\}$ from pigs.

Postal continues, "in the Classical Theory, the object NP of [(1b)] will have an entirely different Deep Structure from that in [(2)], a structure in which the item *pork* itself occurs, together with some nonsyntactic, purely semantic, representation of the meaning, indicating that *pork,* in fact, designates meat from pigs" [124: 107]. In other words, Postal is saying that the underlying representations of (1a) and (1b) are quite different within the standard theory, the former exhibiting at most a relative clause (and at least an NP followed by a PP) and the latter an NP, whereas both (1a) and (1b) would have essentially the same underlying representations within generative semantics. Again, due to restrictions defining deep structure in the standard theory, from a syntactic point of view, *pork* must derive from *pork,* whereas, in generative semantics, *pork* may be derived from syntactic structures which are far more abstract. But this, of course, is the point of the standard theory. Because *pork* is a lexical item, it can be cross-classified or appear in compounds. Thus we find *pork roast, pork sausage,* etc., but not *meat from pigs roast, meat from pigs sausage,* etc. To avoid the latter, generative semantics must invent further ad hoc transformations. To continue, the standard theory predicts that *pork* and *meat from pigs* may exhibit different distributional possibilities. And this is so.

(3) a.   That, my friend, is pork from a pig, not from a hog!
     b.   *That, my friend, is meat from pigs from a pig, not from a hog!

In fact, in the very same article in which Postal expounds on pork, he provides us with a test which we can now use to refute his analysis of *pork.* Recall from the previous chapter that Postal claims that two virtually identical underlying representations of generative semantics have identical contradictory properties. Thus, he claims that the following are contradictory:

(4) a.   I perceive that Larry is similar to Winston Churchill although I perceive that Larry is not similar to Winston Churchill.
     b.   Larry reminds me of Winston Churchill although I perceive that Larry is not similar to Winston Churchill.

As Bowers has shown (cf. section 1.1.1), Postal's claim is false. However, the method can now be applied to *pork:*

(5) a. I perceive that meat from pigs is meat from pigs but I do not perceive that meat from pigs is meat from pigs.
   b. I perceive that meat from pigs is meat from pigs but I do not perceive that pork is meat from pigs.

Here we see that (5a) is indeed contradictory, but (5b) is certainly not. Yet, by applying Postal's own generative semantics criteria which he uses for (4a, b), we see that he is claiming that (5a) and (5b) are both contradictory. This generative semantics test, then, refutes the theory which gave rise to it.

According to the standard theory, items having different deep structures may well exhibit different distributional possibilities in spite of the fact that they may be "essential paraphrases." Such differences are expected within the standard theory which incorporates a level of deep structure and a lexicon, but they are totally unexpected within generative semantics, as Postal's own tests claim.

Since *pork* derives from *meat which comes from pigs* within generative semantics, one expects not to encounter the differences alluded to above. Since there are differences, the theory must scramble to immunize itself against the obvious counterevidence. For example, one should not expect to find differences between *remind* and *strike x as similar,* given generative semantics. But there are differences and some are discovered by Postal more than halfway into his discussion.

(6) a. Max struck me as being similar to Pete in size.
   b. *Max reminded me of Pete in size.

(7) a. Joe struck me as resembling you in weight.
   b. *Joe reminded me of you in weight.

(8) a. Tom struck me as being like Bill in coloring and eyebrow texture.
   b. *Tom reminded me of Bill in coloring and eyebrow texture.

These differences are not to be expected within the generative semantics framework, so new ad hoc theoretical devices are needed to write them off as nondiagnostic. Consider, for example, the scrambling in [124], where a new rule of Property-Factoring, which is never formulated, is proposed along with new conditions. (See Ronat [133] for additional discussion.)

One sees, hopefully, the relevance of deep structure and the lexicon from examples such as those discussed here.

2.2.2 LAKOFF ON INSTRUMENTAL ADVERBS

Lakoff has argued that the following sentences "have the same deep structure" [88]:

(9) a. Seymour sliced the salami with a knife.
     b. Seymour used a knife to slice the salami.

Lakoff does not tell us what underlies (9a) and (9b), nor does he formulate syntactic rules to relate the examples. He simply assumes that it follows from his evidence that all constructions of the following shape are related by deriving from an identical deep structure, whatever that deep structure is:

(10) a. $NP_1 - V - NP_2 - with - NP_3$
      b. $NP_1 - use - NP_3 - to - V - NP_2$

Some examples Lakoff offers in support of this conjecture include the following:

(11) a. Albert $\left\{ \begin{array}{l} *knew \\ computed \end{array} \right\}$ the answer with a slide rule.

      b. Albert used a slide rule to $\left\{ \begin{array}{l} *know \\ compute \end{array} \right\}$ the answer.

(12) a. $\left\{ \begin{array}{l} *The\ explosion \\ John \end{array} \right\}$ killed Harry with dynamite.

      b. $\left\{ \begin{array}{l} *The\ explosion \\ John \end{array} \right\}$ used dynamite to kill Harry.

(13) a. I scratched the wire with a $\left\{ \begin{array}{l} knife \\ *itself \end{array} \right\}$.

      b. I used a knife to scratch $\left\{ \begin{array}{l} the\ wire \\ *itself \end{array} \right\}$.

(14) a. *Melvin broke the window with a chisel with a hammer.
      b. *Melvin used a hammer to use a chisel to break the window.

34

Lakoff argues that the (a) and (b) examples behave similarly with respect to a number of distributional criteria. To block the ungrammatical examples of (11–14) for two different structures, such as (10a) and (10b), would entail a loss of generalization. However, if both (10a) and (10b), and consequently the (a) examples and the (b) examples, respectively, of (11–14) are derived from a single underlying representation, the generalizations could be expressed without proliferation of machinery.

Now, there is a very simple refutation of Lakoff's proposal. He writes: "Let me point out at the outset that [(9a)] and [(9b)] are synonymous." In fact, in view of the theoretical framework Lakoff adopts, it follows from his assumption of a "common deep structure" that such examples must be synonymous. Yet this is just not so, as has been independently remarked by Bresnan [17] and Chomsky [42]. Bresnan notes that the following are not synonymous, as predicted by Lakoff:

(15) a.   All at once Seymour broke the door open with a bat.
     b.   ? All at once Seymour used a bat to break the door open.

(16) a.   Seymour rapidly sliced the salami with a knife.
     b.   ?? Seymour rapidly used a knife to slice the salami.

(17) a.   I did a little slicing with the knife.
     b.   * I did a little using the knife to slice.

Whereas the (b) examples are ungrammatical, or else marginal, the (a) examples are fine. Chomsky also notes pairs which are not synonymous:

(18) a.   John carelessly broke the window with a hammer.
     b.   John carelessly used a hammer to break the window.

(19) a.   John broke the window carelessly with a hammer.
     b.   John used the hammer carelessly to break the window.

Chomsky remarks that the "differences of meaning suggest a difference in the meaning of the sentences from which the adverb is omitted" [42: n. 16], hence a difference in the meaning of sentences having (10a) and (10b). He goes on to note the following counterexamples to Lakoff's proposal:

(20) a.   John used the classroom to propagandize for his favorite doctrines.

      b.   John propagandized for his favorite doctrines with his classroom.

(21)   a.   John used the mallet over and over again to reduce the statue to rubble.

         b.   John reduced the statue to rubble over and over again with the mallet.

(22)   a.   Seymour used this table to write the letter.

         b.   Seymour wrote the letter with this table.

Counterexamples such as Bresnan's and Chomsky's can easily be multiplied. They illustrate quite clearly that the (a) and (b) examples brought to bear by Lakoff are not in fact synonymous. They therefore constitute strong evidence against Lakoff's abstract source for the (10a) and (10b) structures. That there should be similarities in (11–14) is not surprising, for, if (9a) and (9b) "are related by embedding, then one would expect to find partial similarities and some differences," and the differences in sense are manifest "because special semantic properties of *use* are showing up" [17: 368].

    These counterexamples show that (9a) and (9b) do not derive from a "common deep structure." In light of this conclusion, let us consider Lakoff's account of the following:

(23)   a.   *Seymour knew the answer with a slide rule.

         b.   *Seymour used a slide rule to know the answer.

Lakoff's account of the unacceptability of (23b) is summarized in the following quotation:

> . . . the non-occurrence of [(23b)] could be ruled out by a constraint between the verb 'use' and the next lowest verb in the complement sentence. This is a constraint needed elsewhere in English grammar. For example, the verbs *force, remember, try,* etc., require an activity verb in their complements. [88: 14]

Thus, Lakoff argues that (23b) is out for the same reason as are the following (his examples 47–49):

36

(24) a. *I forced John to know the answer.
      b. *I remembered to know the answer.
      c. *I tried to know the answer.

Lakoff concludes: "if something like [(10b)] is the correct deep structure for . . . [(10a)], then no new type of deep structure constraint will have to be added to the theory of grammar to account for the lack of [(23b)]" since the same constraint that rules out (24) can be called upon to rule out (23). However, Lakoff's "generalization" turns out to be a pseudogeneralization.

Lakoff's generalization is that *use,* along with *force, remember,* and *try,* select activity verbs in their embedded complements and that this constraint rules out (23b) as well as (24) (and also (23a) if derived from (23b)). However, as Bresnan notes, by Lakoff's criteria *consider* is an activity verb since it can appear in the embedded complements to *force, remember,* and *try.*

(25) a. I forced John to consider all the alternatives.
      b. I remembered to consider all the alternatives.
      c. I tried to consider all the alternatives.

Therefore, Lakoff's theory predicts that the following should be acceptable, since *use* is alleged to obey the same constraint as *force, remember,* and *try* vis-à-vis activity verbs.

(26) a. *I used a book to consider it (with).
      b. *I used a book to consider slicing the salami (with).

Bresnan points out that (26a, b) are as unacceptable as (23b). This shows that Lakoff's generalization is false. A true generalization would relate (26) and (23b). Lakoff's approach fails to do this.

Bresnan goes on to show that Lakoff's false generalization leads to incorrect predictions concerning (14b), repeated here as (27).

(27) *Melvin used a hammer to use a chisel to break the window.

Since *use* is an activity verb, Lakoff's constraint predicts that (27), and therefore (14a), should be acceptable. This follows from the fact that (28a–c) are acceptable.

(28) a. I forced John to use a hammer.
　　　b. I remembered to use a hammer.
　　　c. I tried to use a hammer.

This, then, is another instance of a false prediction.

　　An explanation for these data would not only relate (23a) and (23b) but also (26a), (26b), and (27). A promising approach to such a generalization has been sketched out by Bresnan [17]. She calls verbs that select instrumental adverbs *I*-verbs. Her explanation for the unacceptability of the relevant sentences is summarized in what she calls Condition *I*.

> Condition *I:* When *use* (and more generally, *use*-verbs) has a verb-phrase complement of a particular type (not an *in order to* clause, but a resultative clause), the embedded verb must be an *I*-type verb. [17: 370]

Within Bresnan's framework, (23a) is ruled out because *know* is not an *I*-verb. That is, *know* is not lexically subcategorized for instrumental adverbs. Example (23b) is ruled out by Condition *I*. Bresnan gives an accurate description of her analysis when she writes that "Condition I is rather natural: it specifies that the result of using an instrument must be something that it is possible to do with an *instrument*." Her explanation for how (9a, b) and (23a, b) are related and distinguished in terms of grammaticality is straightforward: "Condition *I* relates the constructions exemplified in sentences [(9a)] and [(9b)] in a natural way: if [(9a)] were out, then [(9b) would be out, for if [(9a)] were out, *slice* would not be an *I*-type verb." This is indeed the case with (23a) and (23b).

　　Turning now to (26a), we see that Condition *I*, unlike Lakoff's constraint, rules it out automatically, since *consider,* although an activity verb, is not an *I*-verb, as shown by (29).

(29) *I considered it with a book.

In a similar vein, unlike Lakoff's analysis, Bresnan's explains the ungrammaticality of (26b) as a consequence of Condition *I* since (30) is ungrammatical when the adverb is interpreted as instrumental.

(30) *Melvin used it with a chisel.

Bresnan's analysis goes even further. Consider once again the ungrammaticality of (14a), repeated here for convenience:

(31)　*Melvin broke the window with a chisel with a hammer.

Bresnan accounts for the ungrammaticality of (31) by the same means one customarily uses to account for the ungrammaticality of *John called me a taxi a horse, namely, by lexical subcategorization. Just as call is subcategorized so as to select a single direct object, so break is subcategorized so as to select a single instrumental adverb. But according to Lakoff, (31) has a more abstract source and he therefore predicts that (32) is also ungrammatical.

(32)　Melvin used a hammer to break the window with a chisel.

Surprisingly, Lakoff cites (32) and asserts that it is ungrammatical. There is, however, nothing at all deviant about (32). Additional examples bear this remark out:

(33)　a.　Melvin used his brains to cross the ocean with a kayak.
　　　b.　Melvin used his concentration to break the board with a sidekick.
　　　c.　Melvin used his muscles to force the screw with a screwdriver.

Lakoff's analysis predicts that (32) and (33) are ungrammatical, which is a false prediction. Bresnan's analysis, by contrast, appears to predict that they are grammatical, since Condition I is not violated. Here then is one additional example of how a false theory can obscure important distinctions by stating false generalizations.

Lakoff's article is an attack on the concept of deep structure as conceived in the standard theory [36]. He claims to have cast a shadow over deep structure in view of his "results" concerning instrumental adverbs. He claims to have demonstrated that underlying representations must be far more abstract than deep structures in view of the single underlying source for (9a) and (9b). But we have seen here that just the opposite is true. There is in fact evidence to indicate that (9a) and (9b) should have different underlying representations and there is no reason to assume that these are significantly different from the deep structures of [36]. Bresnan's analysis bears this out. Therefore, Lakoff's work on instrumental adverbs should be interpreted as an argument for deep structure.

It cannot be emphasized too strongly that Lakoff gives no underlying structures in his paper on instrumental adverbs, although he asserts that whatever it is, "we need [it] independently." This has been shown to be a specious assertion. Moreover, Chomsky has shown that Lakoff's proposal implies a further loss of generalization, for what could conceivably be the underlying source of the following within Lakoff's framework?

(34)   Albert computed the answer without a slide rule.

Now, (34) obeys the distributional criteria of Lakoff's (11–14):

(35)   a.   *Albert knew the answer without a slide rule.
       b.   *Albert computed the answer without itself.
       c.   *Albert computed the answer without a slide rule without a computer.
       d.   *The explosion killed Harry without dynamite.

Thus, there will be a loss of generalization in Lakoff's framework unless (34) is derived from a more abstract source parallel to his abstract source for (10a). What could the abstract source for (34) be? It could not be (36a), for surely (34) is not synonymous with (36b), which seems to be suggested in Lakoff's framework.

(36)   a.   Albert didn't use a slide rule to compute the answer.
       b.   Albert didn't compute the answer with a slide rule.

In the absence of any specific proposals, we must take (34) as additional evidence against the generative semantics approach.

Lakoff concludes his paper with the remark that "there are fewer grammatical categories and grammatical relations in deep structure than had previously been thought . . . " He describes this result in self-congratulatory terms: "these are rather startling results and even more startling because they were arrived at without the statement of a single rule" [84: 25]. By contrast, Chomsky writes: "I do not see how these questions can be resolved without undertaking an analysis of these structures which *does propose rules as well as underlying structures,* and in this sense, goes well beyond the approach to these questions that Lakoff presents" [43: n. 16].

2.2.3 SUMMATION

The theme of the preceding chapter was "lexical decomposition" and "syntactic irregularity" and there it was argued that, within the framework of generative semantics, the first gives rise to the second. The theme of the present chapter has been the "elimination of deep structure," another touchstone of generative semantics. Yet, it is not difficult to see that these issues are in fact one. For, the growth of syntactic irregularity would not be possible given a restrictive hypothesis such as deep structure, nor would deep structure be possible, given lexical decomposition and exception devices such as generative semantics permits.

In 2.2.1 it was shown that generative semantics actually provides a new source of evidence in support of deep structure and in 2.2.2 it was shown that the alleged arguments against deep structure do not hold. Others have argued for deep structure more directly. For example, Anderson has studied a range of sentences and concluded,

> We have thereby shown that precisely the level of deep structure as defined in the standard theory is the appropriate level to serve as input to the rules of semantic interpretation in this case. If true, this is striking confirmation of the hypothesis about semantic interpretation made by the standard theory: the same level, a level appropriately defined by a context free phrase structure grammar, serves (a) as input to the transformational component; (b) for the statement of selectional and subcategorization restrictions; and (c) as input to the semantic component, at least insofar as that component makes reference to formally defined grammatical relations. [3: 396]

One need not search long in order to locate additional references in which deep structure is said to stand refuted; cf. [102], [111], [151]. But the arguments do not appear to be convincing, and in some cases, e.g. [151], the discussion is even devoid of data. I will therefore content myself here with the foregoing discussion and rest the case on Chomsky's summation:

> There is only one way to provide some justification for a concept that is defined in terms of some general theory, namely, to show that the theory provides revealing explanations for an interesting range of phenomena and that the concept in question plays a role in these explanations. In this sense . . . [deep structure] . . . receives some justification from the linguistic work that is based on grammars of the standard form. [43: 80]

It might be added that a good deal of this justification has been inadvertently provided by generative semantics.

2.3 LOGIC AND SEMANTICS

As deep structure receded from the generative semantics scene, logic was ushered in. Thus, McCawley wrote,

> At the Texas universals conference, Lakoff pointed out that there is much less difference between these supposedly different kinds of representation [semantic and syntactic] than has been hitherto assumed. He observes that there is an almost exact correspondence between the more basic syntactic categories and the primitive terms of symbolic logic and between the rules which he and Ross have proposed as base component universals and the formation rules for symbolic logic . . . [104: 167]

Now what is this astounding correspondence? One example cited by McCawley is the following.

> . . . for example, the relative clause rule NP $\rightarrow$ NP S corresponds to the rule that from a 'term' x and a 'predicate' f one may form the term $\{x:\ f(x)\}$, to be read 'the x's such that $f(x)$' . . .   [104: 167]

Apparently, such remarks are to be considered profound and "startling" but we are never informed as to their relevance either for linguistic theory or for logic, so that there lingers some doubt concerning the relevance of logic to natural language. What correspondence in fact is McCawley talking about when he cites the phrase structure rule NP $\rightarrow$ NP S and his alleged logical rule? Is it that x appears twice and NP twice? But the NP on the left of the phrase structure rule does not play the role of x ! Rather, the NP on the right does, if there is any analogy here at all, and the coreferential NP inside the S, which appears nowhere in the phrase structure rule, is like the x in $f(x)$. Characteristically, McCawley offers no algorithm to go from the "form" of the logical rules to the form of the phrase structure rules, nor does he cite a single fact which is elucidated by appealing to logical notation. Let us all be aware that the dropping of technical terms such as *predicate, function, operator, term,* and so forth is no substitute for genuine empirical advances in linguistics; nor is it evidence that anything of significance is being said.

The correspondence mentioned by McCawley, though never made explicit, is thought to be profound by way of casting light on what semantic representations are. It indicates that "semantic representations can be regarded as trees." This revelation is "startling" because now semantics and syntax are seen to be one. Thus, Postal writes,

> The key feature of this proposal is that syntactic and semantic structures are taken to be homogeneous enough for the mapping between them to be accomplished by a single type of rule, transformations. The homogeneity is, moreover, substantively assumed to mean that both types of structures are representable as labelled bracketings, i.e., trees. [124: 99]

From the point of view of logic, McCawley's, Lakoff's, and Postal's remarks are totally uninteresting. From the point of view of linguistics, they are false. For, they are ultimately based on the evidence adduced in support of the reduction of syntactic categories and the "base component universals" of Ross and Lakoff. Neither of these reductions is empirically justified. The reduction of categories has been described by Bresnan, as noted earlier, as follows: "In what must be regarded as a *tour de force* of reductivism, McCawley chronicles how the syntactic categories fell one after another . . ." [24: 196]. I have already remarked on this chronicle in chapter 1, a chronicle describing the fall of categories such as noun, adjective, preposition, VP, and others. Bresnan has appropriately remarked: "Each of the particular steps McCawley recounts is highly controversial . . ." [24: 197]. It might be added that by now most have been persuasively rebutted. As for the "base component universals," they are simply vacuous.[1]

In what sense do generative semanticists claim to have made progress in semantics? They claim to have accounted for paraphrase relations and synonymy. Thus, Lakoff claims to have accounted for the "synonymy" of the following pair:

(37) a. Seymour sliced the salami with a knife.
      b. Seymour used a knife to slice the salami.

And Postal claims to have accounted for the "paraphrase" relations of the *remind* and *strike-like,* and so forth. But abundant evidence shows that (37a) and (37b) are not synonymous, that *remind* and *strike-like* examples are not paraphrases in any clear sense, etc. It is therefore misleading, and to some extent irresponsible, to offer false analyses as progress toward an explication of whatever semantic relations may hold between the aforementioned examples. Nor does the use of such phrases as "virtual synonymy," "essential paraphrase," etc., contribute to our understanding of semantics.

In conclusion, it cannot be conceded that anything is gained by adopting the object language of symbolic logic as a syntactic or semantic basis for natural language. Indeed, what evidence is currently available suggests just the opposite.

NOTES TO CHAPTER 2

[1] The reader is particularly directed to the excellent critique by Schachter [146] for a detailed demonstration of the poverty of the generative semantics program of reductionism and to [119] for a discussion of the vacuousness of their universal base hypothesis.

Chapter 3

Deus ex Machina: Semantic Predicates and Global Rules

The content of a concept diminishes as its extension increases; if its extension becomes all-embracing, its content must vanish altogether.

Gottlob Frege

. . . it is often a step forward . . . when linguistic theory becomes more complex, more articulated and refined . . . it is misleading to say that a better theory is one with a more limited conceptual structure, and that we prefer the minimal conceptual elaboration, the least theoretical apparatus. Insofar as this notion is comprehensible, it is not in general correct. . . . One who takes the more "conservative" stance, maintaining only that a grammar is a set of conditions on derivations, has no burden of proof to bear because he is saying virtually nothing.

Noam Chomsky

I have proposed that rules of grammar be considered as well-formedness conditions on derivations (or 'derivational constraints'). In the most general case, rules of grammar will be global in nature. Phrase structure rules and transformations turn out to be special cases of derivational constraints. From the point of view of linguistic description, the theory of derivational constraints is as much an innovation over transformational grammar as transformational grammar was over phrase structure grammar.

George Lakoff

3.1 THEORETICAL PROPHYLACTIC AND VACUOUS GENERALITY

In discussing Adlerian and Freudian psychology, Popper [121] argues that their apparent strength is in their weakness, that these psychological theories cannot be considered scientific theories because they cannot be refuted. All conceivable test cases can be interpreted and explained away in either theory. This artifice of immunization is, according to Popper, what distinguishes a prescientific or pseudoscientific theory from genuine science.

45

It is not my purpose here to extend the philosophical discussion. However, I do want to argue that generative semantics has a certain affinity with
the two examples discussed by Popper. In particular, I think it is reasonably clear that generative semantics, by adopting various devices, has
succeeded in immunizing itself to such an extent that it has become
virtually irrefutable. One can certainly argue against generative semantics,
but as a consequence of devices such as semantic predicates and global
rules, it is not possible in principle to falsify it.

3.2 SEMANTIC PREDICATES

Let us first consider the device of semantic predicates. By way of
example, consider Postal's final proposal for deriving sentences such as
Larry reminds me of Winston Churchill.

(1)   STRIKE x(me) [SIMILAR y(Larry) z(W.C.)] $\Longrightarrow$ Raising
      STRIKE x(me) y(Larry)[SIMILAR z(W.C.)] $\Longrightarrow$ Predicate-Raising
      STRIKE SIMILAR x(me) y(Larry) z(W.C.) $\Longrightarrow$ Psych-Movement
      STRIKE SIMILAR y(Larry) x(me) z(W.C.) $\Longrightarrow$ Subject-Formation
      y(Larry) STRIKE SIMILAR x(me) z(W.C.) $\Longrightarrow$ Lexical Insertion
      and Variable Substitution

Larry reminds me Winston Churchill.

Working backwards, the first thing to be noticed is that the correct surface
structure is not generated in view of the absence of the preposition *of*.
Postal is aware of this fact, but apparently assumes that it is mere detail. In
fact, however, the absence of *of* in underlying representations leads to
additional ad hoc features, a point made repeatedly in chapter 2 of this
book. Generative semanticists, in general, have it that details pose no
problems and Postal's analysis is no exception in this respect. In the
absence of an explicit proposal, however, this assumption cannot be
granted.
   A second observation is that Postal has utilized McCawley's rule of
Subject-Formation, although he nowhere formulates it (nor does McCawley). This rule leads to further difficulties, as noted at the beginning of
chapter 1 in connection with Berman's criticism of it. As for Psych-
Movement, there is no convincing evidence in support of it and what little
evidence has been advanced in its support by Postal in [126: chap. 6] has

been countered by Ruwet in [144: chap. 5]. As for Predicate-Raising, this putative rule has never been motivated, and it has been shown to lead to false predictions in connection with causatives (see section 1.1.3). Moreover, Predicate-Raising is conceived as an optional rule. But what happens if it does not apply in the course of (1)? Then (2) is derived.

(2)   Larry strikes me similar Winston Churchill.

But (2) is not *Larry strikes me as being similar to Winston Churchill*. In fact (2) is ungrammatical. Are we again to believe that items such as *as, being,* and *to* can be trivially predicted? In the absence of any explicit proposals, again, such an assumption is gratuitous.

These observations are more than sufficient to suggest that Postal's analysis of *remind* is not in fact a serious proposal. The additional empirical considerations brought to bear in section 1.1 above support this conclusion. And, as has been observed by others, there are further questions raised by the abstract analysis of *remind*. For example, Postal argues that SIMILAR is logically a symmetric predicate and that therefore (3a) and (3b) have identical truth conditions. It should then follow from his analysis, as noted by Leben [97], that (4a) and (4b) have identical truth conditions.

(3)   a.   Max is similar to Pete.
       b.   Pete is similar to Max.
(4)   a.   Max reminds me of Pete.
       b.   Pete reminds me of Max.

But this prediction is false. Sentence (4a) can be false when (4b) is true and vice versa.

Ample evidence has been provided to seriously impugn the *strike-like* analysis of *remind*. In particular, it has been shown that there are differences between *strike similar* and *remind* clauses, that they are not synonymous. It is to the discredit of generative semantics that no such evidence can be considered as crucial. This irrefutability trait of generative semantics is in part a consequence of its incorporation of "semantic predicates" of the type typically presented in capital letters. It is conveniently summarized by Postal as follows:

> The idea is that the underlying elements are *semantic* verbs, that is, predicates. Consequently, the claim is only that the underlying ele-

ments of *remind* clauses are those predicates which are lawfully connected to the various regularities documented for *strike* and Similarity Predicates. In particular, I would like to emphasize that it is not excluded that the actual lexical verb *strike* may have certain special properties not associated with the underlying predicate or predicate complex which shows up as the Surface Verb *remind*. [124: 114]

Notice here the implication that generative semantics is irrefutable. He is saying: show me a counterexample and it is not one because *remind* and *strike-like* differ and the semantic or syntactic differences can be attributed to the "Surface Verb" *remind*. This immunization against refutation is another reason for rejecting the theory that gave rise to it.[1]

3.3   GLOBAL RULES

Although generative semanticists apparently recognize that there is some point to constraining theories of natural language, in practice this fundamental point is neglected. It may therefore be of value to clarify the fundamental goal of linguistics by drawing on an extended quotation from Chomsky.

> The fundamental problem of linguistic theory . . . is to account for the choice of a particular grammar, given the data available to the language-learner. To account for this inductive leap, linguistic theory must try to characterize a fairly narrow class of grammars that are available to the language learner; it must, in other words, specify the notion "human language" in a narrow and restrictive fashion. A "better theory," then, is one that specifies the class of possible grammars so narrowly that some procedure of choice or evaluation can select a descriptively adequate grammar for each language from this class . . . . Given alternative linguistic theories that meet this condition, we might compare them in terms of general "simplicity" or other metatheoretic notions, but it is unlikely that such considerations will have any more significance within linguistics than they do in any other field. *For the moment, the problem is to construct a general theory of language that is so richly structured and so restrictive in the conditions it imposes that, while meeting the condition of descriptive adequacy, it can sufficiently narrow the class of grammars so that the problem of choice of grammar (and explanation, in some serious sense) can be approached.* [43: 125; emphasis mine. MKB]

Generative semantics, as a theory of natural language, has provided us with ample illustrations (cf. chapter 2) of the extent to which the standard theory succeeds in fulfilling Chomsky's desiderata. (Recall that the standard theory eliminates many of the generative semantics analyses by virtue of its incorporation of a level of deep structure.)

Perhaps another illustration will help to make the point. Within the framework of the standard theory, it is assumed that syntactic rules, as well as phonological rules, are ordered according to the following principle:

> Rules are applied in linear order, each rule operating on the string as modified by all earlier applicable rules. [46]

This principle of ordering is restrictive in the sense that it eliminates many imaginable derivations and conditions that might otherwise be associated with syntactic and phonological rules. For example, it excludes the following:

(5) Apply R_j to phrase marker A only if R_i has already applied.
(6) Apply R_j to phrase marker A only if A is B in underlying representations.
(7) Apply R_i to phrase marker A only if R_j will later apply.

Statements such as (5–7) have been called "global rules." To illustrate a proposed global rule, I will briefly discuss an example from the phonology of Lardil, cited in Kisseberth [84]. According to Kisseberth, Lardil exhibits a rule dropping word-final vowels in words of three or more syllables. There is a second rule dropping word-final nonapical consonants.

(8) a. $V \rightarrow \emptyset \ / \ VC_1VC_1\underline{\quad\quad}\#$

b. $\begin{bmatrix} C \\ -\text{apical} \end{bmatrix} \rightarrow \emptyset \ / \ \underline{\quad\quad}\#$

Given an underlying form such as *ŋawuŋawu* in Lardil, by ordering rule (a) before rule (b), we expect the following derivation in the standard theory:

(9) *ŋawuŋawu*
ŋawuŋaw   RULE (a)
ŋawuŋa   RULE (b)

We might ask why it is that (a) does not reapply to give *ŋawuŋ*, which would then be followed by a second application of (b), yielding **ŋawu*. In other words, what blocks the following derivation?

(10)   *ŋawuŋawu*
       ŋawuŋaw   RULE (a)
       ŋawuŋa   RULE (b)
       ŋawuŋ   RULE (a)
       ŋawu   RULE (b)

Within the standard theory, rules are linearly ordered, and by the definition of linear order, rules are precluded from reapplying. Now let us turn to generative semantics which allows global rules. According to Kisseberth, "phonological rules must be 'global' in nature—that is, the conditions which determine whether or not a pair of adjacent lines in a derivation are properly related by a given rule must refer not just to the pair of lines in question, but to other aspects of the derivation in which they occur as well." In other words, rules such as (5–7) are allowed. Postal also remarks that "there exist global filters, those whose statement requires reference to multiple levels of structure within a derivation, that is, to more than one tree" [128]. And Lakoff states that "the trouble with phrase-structure and transformational rules is that they are local; they define well-formedness conditions on individual phrase-markers and on pairs of successive phrase-markers in a derivation."

Now let us see how such a theory accounts for Lardil *ŋawuŋa* from underlying *ŋawuŋawu*. Lakoff tells us that "there is every reason to believe that they [global rules] will allow one to get rid of the unprincipled [*sic*] blocking device of extrinsic rule-ordering" [91: 83] and Kisseberth claims that it is possible to dispense with ordering in this case by adopting "a global condition on apocope" to the effect that "the deleting vowel be in word-final position underlyingly." This global condition would prevent the undesired derivation given in (10) because at the stage *ŋawuŋa*, where word-final *a* would otherwise be expected to drop, we look back to the most abstract stage and see that this *a* is not word-final. Thus, the desired *ŋawuŋa* is generated.

Already at this rudimentary level of discussion, we witness the superiority of the standard theory to the theory of generative semantics incorporating global rules. For, given (8a) and (8b), consider the relative power of the two theories. The standard theory allows ordering conditions satisfying linearity; generative semantics allows global rules satisfying no well-defined criteria. The standard theory allows for two possible languages, one in which (8a) is ordered before (8b), which is identical to Lardil, where *ŋawuŋawu* gives rise to *ŋawuŋa*, and one in which (8a) is ordered after (8b), where *ŋawuŋawu* gives rise to *ŋawuŋaw*. The standard theory predicts that both languages are possible natural languages. However, the possibility of deriving *ŋawu* from *ŋawuŋawu* by means of derivation (10) is ruled out by the standard theory as a consequence of linear ordering. By contrast, generative semantics allows for many conceivable languages. For example, by imposing Kisseberth's global rule on (8a), we get (9). And by associating a global condition with (8b) to the effect that the deleting consonant be in word-final position underlyingly, we get *ŋawuŋaw* from *ŋawuŋawu*. Further, by associating no global conditions at all, generative semantics allows the possibility of (10)! By adopting different global rules, we get still more possibilities.[2] It is therefore easy to see that, given a fixed set of rules, generative semantics can express all the possibilities permitted by the standard theory and more. Thus, the standard theory, unlike generative semantics, makes some headway towards accounting for the "inductive leap" of the language-learner by excluding hypotheses that he or she would otherwise have to make given a theory incorporating global rules.

There is, moreover, a second fact worthy of remarking in connection with the Lardil example. It is simply that the standard theory rules out (10) by a universal condition on the form of grammars.[3] This it does for Lardil as for any conceivable language. By contrast, (10) is eliminated in the case of Lardil under the theory of generative semantics by a condition, i.e., a global rule, which is ad hoc to Lardil. Kisseberth himself recognizes the difference in this regard when he writes,

> The first alternative [linear ordering of the standard theory] obviously claims that the failure of apocope to affect *ŋawuŋa* is the result of a universal principle, while the latter [global rule of generative semantics] alternative attributes this failure to a language-particular constraint on apocope. The first alternative is consequently a much stronger position and is the one that has generally been maintained. . . ." [84: 420]

It is therefore surprising that Kisseberth concludes that "in any case, the problem posed by *ŋawuŋa* does not appear to require extrinsic ordering statements in a grammar" [84: 421] and that Lakoff [91] views this as confirmation of the global theory. Again, we see that generative semantics, by adopting global rules, fails to satisfy the fundamental desideratum of linguistic theory and is therefore a step backward.

> . . . it is often a step forward . . . when linguistic theory becomes more complex, more articulated and refined—a point that has been noted repeatedly. . . . For example, it is a step forward when we complicate linguistic theory by distinguishing among all imaginable rules the two categories "transformational rules" and "phonological rules," with their specific properties, and formulate conditions on their application and interrelation. [43: 126]

Evidently generative semanticists place a premium on maximal generality, without, however, heeding Frege's observation that "the content of a concept diminishes as its extension increases; if its extension becomes all-embracing, its content must vanish altogether." This point, echoed in Chomsky's remarks, is so obvious that it hardly deserves extended discussion. And yet it seems to be at the root of the generative semantics dilemma. Even in such an established field as mathematics, the relevance of the point is commonplace and has been remarked. For example, Mac-Lane has noted that the development of category theory illustrates that "good general theory does not search for the maximum generality, but for the right generality" [101: 103] and Menger has remarked that a "thorough examination of science and mathematics reveals that . . . many ideas have merged and lost their identity in misconceptions." According to Menger, "what contemporary mathematics calls for is not so much a razor as a device that analyzes mixtures and isolates their various components" [108: 415–416]. Tisza also recognizes the problem when he responds, "It would seem that the need for such a prism in physics is still more pressing" [155: 56]. In linguistics, as in mathematics and other fields, one must distinguish generalizations from significant generalizations. This important distinction seems to have been missed by proponents of generative semantics.[4]

As Chomsky has indicated, success in the task of accounting for the language acquirer's "inductive leap" will inevitably lead to the introduction of distinctions and refinements into the theory, examples of which include *deep structure, linear ordering of rules, the transformational cycle,* and many others. To the extent that such devices eliminate hypotheses that would otherwise be made by the language-learner, while remaining consistent with the data, they must be considered as steps forward; to the extent that such devices entail a loss of linguistically significant generalization, they must be rejected.[5] It is simply perverse to conclude on vague grounds of parsimony, i.e., Occam's razor, that theories eliminating deep structure, the cycle, ordering, etc., are to be favored over the standard theory.

The point has been clearly drawn by others. For example, Ruwet notes,

> Lakoff seems to see in the introduction of the notion of global constraints a meaningful generalization and simplification, but this idea is misleading. It should be seen, in fact, that the general admission of global constraints amounts to a considerable augmentation of the descriptive power of the grammar: a grammar with this power seems to be capable of describing nearly anything. [145]

A second, more empirically based criticism of global rules is the observation that the data which form the basis for their alleged motivation, when expanded, demonstrate that the putative generalizations are in fact spurious. I have sighted some instances of spurious generalizations in chapter 2, e.g., Lakoff's discussion of instrumental adverbs, but we can now turn to a case involving global rules. Lakoff [91] proposes the following global rule:

(11)   No single lexical item may take a *for-to* complementizer and undergo both the passive transformation and Equi-NP deletion. [91: 633]

Lakoff illustrates this global rule with the following examples:

(12) a.   Minnie desired to kick Sam in the shins.
      b.   *To kick Sam in the shins was desired by Minnie.

(13) a.   Sam tried to escape from America.
      b.   *To escape from America was tried by Sam.

(14) a.   Sarah expected to have a party the following day.
      b.   *To have a party the following day was expected by Sarah.

It has been noted, however, in [8], that Equi-NP Deletion has nothing at all to do with the ungrammaticality of the (b) examples of (12–14), as indicated by (15–16).

(15) a. We should like for John to go.
      b. *For John to go would be liked by us.

(16) a. We would prefer for John to be examined by a competent
          doctor.
      b. *For John to be examined by a competent doctor would be
          preferred by us.

The simple observation is that infinitival phrases such as those in (12–14)
are not NP's (noun phrases) and therefore should not be expected to
passivize. This position has been argued at length in [54] and [55] by
Emonds; cf. also Milsark [109]. Lakoff's case for (11), therefore, simply
collapses. The mistake is due, on the one hand, to a disregard for a wide
range of data, including (15–16), and, on the other, to the postulation of
otiose and, in this case, pernicious, categories such as NP for infinitival
phrases.

In [91] Lakoff takes credit for global devices when he writes, "we
require a theory of global grammar. . . . This is as much an innovation over
transformational grammar as transformational grammar is over phrase
structure grammar" [91: 638]. Actually, a universal global device had
been suggested as early as 1960 by Lees in [98]; cf. section 6.2 of this text
for discussion. But it is true that Lakoff should receive credit for advocating language-specific global rules. It is of some interest that all of the
examples offered in support of global rules in [91] have been discussed and
given a nonglobal treatment in [8]. This rejoinder has in turn sparked a
reply by Lakoff [93], but the latter does not discuss the criticism directed
against [91]. Rather, Lakoff raises the discussion to an abstract
metatheoretical level and attempts to score points by caricaturing two of the
proposed alternatives to global rules as "ad hoc coding mechanisms using
arbitrary grammatical elements" [93: 76]. Now the fate of global rules will
ultimately be decided on the basis of specific cases, not on a priori
conceptions of what is arbitrary and what natural; Lakoff's failure to
respond to the criticisms of [8] can only be interpreted as a recognition of
the weakness of global rules as a serious proposal for the explanation of the
range of facts adduced in [91], e.g., those listed in (12–14). Nevertheless,
it may be worthwhile to investigate Lakoff's critique of the two proposals
found in [8], which he characterizes as "ad hoc coding mechanisms using
arbitrary grammatical elements."[6]

Consider, first, the discussion of auxiliary-reduction. To set the discussion in proper perspective, it is necessary to review King's observations to the effect that the rules of English which reduce and contract auxiliaries do not generally apply if the following element is removed by deletion or movement.

(17) a. Joan's taken more from you than Bill $\left\{ {}_{*'\text{S}}^{\text{has}} \right\}$ _____ from me.

  b. You'll need some and I $\left\{ {}_{*'\text{ll}}^{\text{will}} \right\}$ _____ too.

  c. I wonder where Gerald $\left\{ {}_{*'\text{S}}^{\text{is}} \right\}$ _____ today.

  d. We told him what a big boy you $\left\{ {}_{*'\text{re}}^{\text{are}} \right\}$ _____ today.

Lakoff redescribes this situation with a global rule:

(18) If, at any point in the syntax, a constituent immediately following *be* is deleted, then, later in the phonology, that *be* cannot undergo stress-lowering (and subsequent contraction). [91: 632]

According to Lakoff, (18) is a global rule because "we have a constraint operating at two separate points in the grammar." For Lakoff's global rule to be observationally adequate with respect to (17), it is of course necessary to replace *be* in (18) with a more general characterization of the class of contracting or stress-lowering elements.

A nonglobal approach to these facts is suggested in [8]. This proposal is embodied in the following quote:

(19) any language-particular rule which moves or deletes constituents leaves a special boundary symbol at the site of the missing constituent, and particular phonological rules may then be blocked by the presence of this boundary within the domain of the rule. [8: 79]

Let us now consider Lakoff's a priori dismissal of (19).

The only function of this device [boundary symbol] is to code the fact that certain phonological rules are sensitive to the occurrence of certain syntactic rules at some distant earlier point in the derivation. [93: 79]

Thus, Lakoff considers (19) a trick, a failure to face up to the global character of contraction in English. He goes on to question the existence of the boundary symbol:

> Again a new grammatical element (the 'special symbol') appears. The implicit claim is made that this new element characterizes a real category distinction. Again, the stock of grammatical categories is increased by an arbitrary category, and the naturalness of the description is correspondingly decreased. [93: 79]

Lakoff thus considers (19) to be an "arbitrary coding device," a trick, which unnecessarily increases the stock of theoretical devices. But notice that (19) is a proposed universal, applying not just to English, but to all natural languages. It therefore represents a serious attempt at constraining the form of grammars. By contrast, Lakoff's (18) is a language-specific rule. It is not universal. Indeed it applies only to English since it mentions English lexical items such as *be*. Other languages could have similar rules or not. Thus, Lakoff's proposal is "destructuring." It does not limit the class of conceivable grammars. Thus, even though (18) and (19) might have the same effect for the specific case of English, the universal proposal (19) must be favored; it can be falsified by simply finding a counterexample in any of the world's languages. The same cannot be said of (18). Thus, (19) has consequences and can be judged in terms of these. But (18) may or may not be present in the grammar of a language and is accordingly ad hoc in the real sense of the word.

Now, certainly all explicit proposals are in some sense coding devices. For example, if Lakoff's global rule (18) were ever made explicit, i.e., formalized, it is far from clear that it would not contain some "tag" such as that which Lakoff so vehemently inveighs against.[7] Before jumping so readily to an a priori assessment of (19) as arbitrary, however, let us proceed in the usual manner of rational inquiry. In order to get anywhere, one must make a proposal. As a general heuristic, it is best to formulate proposals within a reasonably explicit framework. We have only one such framework—that of the standard theory. The next move, not undertaken in [8], would be to see if there is any independent support for (19), or alternatively, if (19) could be shown to follow from more basic properties of the theory, in this case, the standard theory. Now, the feasibility of this heuristic procedure is borne out by the fact that in a recent serious study of contraction and reduction phenomena in English and French, Selkirk [150] has attempted to show that (19) is not an unnatural formulation within the framework of the standard theory. She points out that Chomsky and Halle had already provided some justification for a rule inserting word boundaries (cf. [46]) and that this justification was based on phonological considerations. Selkirk has revised this independently needed rule and formulated the following more general convention in place of (19):

(20)   Traces Convention: Transformations which move or delete constituents do not move or delete the word boundaries associated with these constituents. [150: 15]

Selkirk notes that "the boundary symbols left behind by transformations (I will call them *traces*) are not new ad-hoc devices." She points out that "they are independently required and always have been included in the standard theory" [150: 16]. Her approach to contraction phenomena in English quite clearly goes beyond (19), but nevertheless, is sympathetic to it. Moreover, it completely cuts the ground out from under Lakoff's objections.

Selkirk shows even more. She provides a strong diagnostic test empirically distinguishing Lakoff's global rule (18) from her nonglobal Traces Convention (20):

In this case, "global rule" is simply another name for a descriptive statement. The formulation has no explanatory value, and, moreover, it is false as it stands. This global rule [(18)] claims (erroneously) that the *be* in *So is Thelma,* and *Who is John?,* which at one point in their derivations most certainly did precede a deletion site, couldn't undergo stress-lowering and contraction. But one finds *So's Thelma* and *Who's John?*. The theory of global rules in no way predicts this. The Monosyllable Rule, accompanied by a theory of traces, does predict this. Obviously, only when *be* precedes traces left by the deletion or movement of a constituent will it fail to be subject to the Monosyllable Rule. When *be* is moved away from the traces, it is free from their influence. [150: 94]

Thus, Selkirk's nonglobal approach to contraction phenomena predicts that *So's Thelma* and *Who's John?* are possible contracted sequences in English, whereas, by contrast, Lakoff's global rule (18) predicts that they are not. On the basis of this empirical distinction, then, it is obvious that the nonglobal approach to the data, once again, wins out, and that the global rule proposed by Lakoff must be dismissed as a serious proposal.

In addition to the empirical arguments favoring Selkirk's approach to contraction, once again the obvious but important point can be made that Selkirk's Traces Convention (20) is a proposed universal, whereas Lakoff's global rule (18) is language-specific. In this sense, the claims made by Selkirk are far more interesting. Selkirk's approach can be tested against languages other than English, whereas the same cannot be said of Lakoff's global rule.

As with semantic predicates, it is again possible to illustrate how generative semantics immunizes itself against refutation by incorporating global rules. For, although the foregoing observations argue against global rules, and hence generative semantics, the latter can never be refuted since the global rules can always be revised ad hoc so as to read " . . . except . . . " For example, Selkirk's counterevidence can be written off by revising (18) with the ad hoc "except" codicil. Thus, global rules constitute a new mechanism for the growth of irregularity in generative semantics. This, together with its prophylactic qualities, therefore provides an additional argument against generative semantics.

Let us now turn to the second nonglobal analysis offered in [8] and characterized by Lakoff as one more of the "ad hoc coding mechanisms using arbitrary grammatical elements." This case involves Greek case assignment for which a global formulation is provided by Lakoff in [91] and Andrews in [4]. In response to Lakoff's formulation, [8] offers a nonglobal alternative in terms of indices with the caveat: "we leave open the question of whether this principle actually gives a correct account of case agreement in Greek until a more detailed examination of a wide range of Greek sentences is undertaken." In the meanwhile, a detailed examination of a wide range of Greek data has been undertaken by Quicoli in [131] with the following conclusion:

> . . . the force of some facts listed as counter-examples in Andrews [4] was greatly underestimated in Andrews' own analysis, and totally ignored in Lakoff [91] [93]. . . . once the facts are properly examined a different analysis, much closer to earlier traditional grammarian's insights, will result, and . . . this analysis supports the theory of transformational grammar as outlined in Chomsky [36] and argues against the 'global derivational constraint' hypothesis advocated in Andrews [4] and in Lakoff [91], [93].

Let us here consider some of the reasons for Quicoli's rejection of Lakoff's global rule, which is repeated as (21):

(21)   In surface structure, an adjective or participle must agree in case with the noun phrase that was its derived subject at the end of the first cycle on the innermost S containing that adjective or participle. [91: 629]

Since this rule mentions two distinct stages of the derivation, it is a global rule. Now Andrews [4] also formulates a global rule for the Greek data:

(22)   A predicate modifier agrees with the NP which was its subject at the end of the first cycle applying to that predicate modifier. [4: 147]

The difference between (21) and (22) is that (22) mentions "predicate modifiers," including adjectives, participles, and predicate nouns, whereas (21) fails to include predicate nouns. Quicoli notes, "the reason for restricting the rule in this way, although not mentioned in Lakoff [91], [93], is apparently to avoid some facts listed as counter-examples in Andrews' analysis," but this difference need not concern us here. Rather, let us consider the implications of (21) when confronted by concrete examples. (Henceforth I draw heavily on Quicoli's critique of Lakoff and Andrews.)

(23)   *Kurou   edeonto   hōs prothumotatou genesthai*
        Cyrus-GEN begged-3PL as   devoted-GEN   to-be
        'They begged Cyrus to be as devoted as possible.'

In (23) we see that 'Cyrus' and 'devoted' are both in the genitive case. Lakoff and Andrews adopt a deep structure something like (24).

(24)   [They begged Cyrus [Cyrus be as devoted]$_{S_1}$]$_{S_0}$

The instance of 'Cyrus' in the matrix sentence is marked for the genitive as required by the verb 'begged'. But what about the predicate modifier 'devoted', which is also genitive? If Equi-NP Deletion deletes the embedded instance of 'Cyrus', there will be no subject, and Lakoff's global rule (21) will be inapplicable, leaving 'devoted' with no case. In [93], his response to [8], Lakoff does not comment on this observation; however, in [94] Lakoff asserts that Equi-NP Deletion is to be formulated not as a deletion process but with the "superimposing of the vanishing NP over the triggering NP." This suggestion is reflected in (25) and also suggested by Andrews in [4].

(25)   [They begged Cyrus [Cyrus be as devoted] s_1] s_0

Quicoli's remarks in response to (25) are to the point.

> This immediately raises numerous questions. First of all, the observable *fact* in the case of sentence [(23)] is that the predicate modifier *prothumotatou* 'devoted-GEN' is *Genitive,* in agreement with the NP *Kurou* 'Cyrus-GEN' which is the the surface structure *object* of the matrix S—i.e., with the NP object of *edeonto* 'begged-3PL' which is a verb that requires *Genitive* objects. . . . It should be then an uncontroversial matter that the burden of the proof in this case is not on someone claiming that the predicate modifier in [(23)] is agreeing with the object of the matrix, but rather on someone making a different claim. Since Andrews and Lakoff make one such claim, it is incumbent upon them to prove that the predicate modifier in [(23)] is, in fact, agreeing with the 'cyclic subject' superimposed on the object, and not simply with the object of the matrix. Unless this is proved, if it can be proved at all, Andrews' and Lakoff's contention that predicate modifiers agree with their 'cyclic subject' remains a purely arbitrary claim. [131: 213–14]

Quicoli continues with the following observations:

> There is a second question which is even more serious. One of the main justifications for postulating *global rules* (cf. Lakoff [91], [94]; Postal [128]) has been the claim that *global rules* would permit the elimination of 'coding mechanisms' which 'encode' properties of the derivation at the stage of the transformational cycle to keep them available at postcyclical stages.
> Now, Andrews' and Lakoff's "superimposition" is precisely one such 'coding mechanism': the EQUI rule is modified for the sole purpose of 'coding information' during the stage of the transformational cycle to make it available at postcyclical stages when the *Case Agreement* rule can make crucial use of it. Their proposal and a proposal involving a 'coding mechanism' are thus indistinguishable.

Furthermore, it is an *arbitrary* 'coding mechanism', since . . . there is no external evidence to support their modification of the EQUI rule as a process of superimposition of the complement subject on its 'controller'. [131: 214–15]

Quicoli concludes,

> . . . we have here an instance where the postulation of a *global rule* far from eliminating recourse to 'coding mechanisms', would, in fact, depend *crucially* on the existence of one such mechanism. Hence, the reasons for postulating a *global rule* in order to avoid 'coding devices', at least in this particular case, are simply non-existent. [131: 215]

Consider now the following sentence cited by Quicoli:

(26)   a.   *sumbouleuō soi   prothumōi einai*
           advise-1SG you-DAT zealous-DAT to-be
           'I advise you to be zealous.'

        b.   *sumbouleuō soi   prothumon einai*
           advise-1SG you-DAT zealous-ACC to-be
           'I advise you to be zealous.'

Either of (26) is possible in Classical Greek, and Andrews cites several such examples, noting that cases such as (26b) are exceptions to his global rule. (Lakoff cites no such examples.) Andrews attempts to account for such examples by conjecturing that one "may merely say that agreement has failed to operate at all" [4: 149]. When agreement "fails to operate," the unmarked modifier goes into the accusative. However, as Quicoli observes, Andrews' analysis, and Lakoff's as well, must then incorporate the following new devices:

(27)   a.   A mechanism optionally blocking the global rule so as to provide for the nonoccurrence of the dative case for the modifier in (26b).
        b.   A rule assigning unmarked modifiers the accusative case.

The effects of (27) are represented diagrammatically as follows:

(28)   ... [... V – NP – [... Y ... Pred. Modifier]]
                (a) |_____×_____| (b) ↓
                                              ACC

The failure of (27), and the global approach in general, is clarified by the following relevant examples provided by Quicoli:

(29) a *sunoida*   *emautōi*   *eu*   *poiēsas*
        am-aware-of   myself-DAT   well   having-done-NOM
        'I am aware that I have done well.'

     b. *sunoida*   *emautōi*   *eu*   *poiēsanti*
        am-aware-of   myself-DAT   well   having-done-DAT
        'I am aware that I have done well.'

Lakoff and Andrews take the predicate modifier in (29b) to agree with the "superimposed cyclic subject." Lakoff fails to mention examples such as (29a), but Andrews is aware that they pose problems for the global approach. How is the nominative of the predicate modifier of (29a) to be derived? Andrews suggests that the rule of EQUI be able to superimpose the embedded subject on either the subject or the object of (29). In case it superimposes the embedded subject on the matrix object, we derive (29b) after the global rule applies. In case it substitutes the embedded subject for the matrix subject, we derive (29a) after the global rule applies. Thus, in addition to the new devices listed in (27), Andrews and Lakoff require the following theoretical elaboration:

(30) EQUI superimposes the embedded subject on the controller object or the controller subject.

This suggestion is represented diagrammatically as:

(31) [I am aware I [I having-done well]]
       ↑_____↑ |

The problem with (30) is that it is false. Not only is the "superimposition" unjustified, as noted in the foregoing quotes, but (30) leads to false predictions in connection with other examples.

62

(32) a. *lanthanō*   *emauton*   *poiōn*   *ti*
          I-escaped-notice-of   myself-ACC doing-NOM something

      'I escaped notice of myself doing something.'

      b. *lanthanō   *emauton*   *poiounta*   *ti*
          I-escaped-notice-of   myself-ACC doing-ACC something

As Quicoli notes, (32b) is impossible. Yet, by allowing the embedded subject to substitute for either the controller object, or the controller subject, Andrews and Lakoff predict that (32b) is acceptable. Since this is false, EQUI will have to be subjected to further theoretical elaboration.

(33) EQUI superimposes the embedded subject of predicates such as *sunoida* for the controller object or the controller subject and for the controller subject alone in the case of predicates such as *lanthano*.

Clearly, something is being missed by such an account of Greek. Global rules, like the exception devices discussed in chapter 1, lead to the growth of irregularity. An explanation for these facts would have the ungrammaticality of (32b) not as an ad hoc statement, but as a consequence of more general properties of Greek syntax. Such is indeed the consequence of Quicoli's nonglobal approach.

Quicoli notes that there is still a further difficulty with the global approach. Given a device such as (27a), one expects this blocking mechanism to be relevant to structures underlying (29) and (32). That is, the global rule should optionally apply to these structures. When it optionally fails to apply, we expect to encounter the following as a consequence of (27b):

(34) a. *sunoida   myself-DAT pred. modifier-ACC
      b. *lanthano myself-ACC pred. modifier-ACC (= (32b))

But (34a) and (34b) are impossible. (Notice that (33) therefore does not successfully block (32b).) Since the global theory predicts that they are possible, we see that still further theoretical accretions will be needed—a device to block the blocking of the global rule, i.e., to block (27a).

"At this point, I find it quite superfluous to present further negative evidence," writes Quicoli. He continues, "The bulk of counterevidence so far is more than sufficient to prove, beyond any reasonable doubt, that

Lakoff's and Andrews' analyses are observationally inadequate in fundamental respects and we must reject the analyses as a requisite for meeting the lower level of *observational adequacy.*"

The global approach makes many false predictions and is a breeding ground for syntactic irregularity. By contrast, the ungrammaticality of (34) follows quite naturally from Quicoli's nonglobal analysis which uses indices.

It is tempting to punctuate this section with a brief look at yet one further consequence of Lakoff's global rules as formulated in [91]. The observation is due to Barone [9] and relates to Lakoff's global rule of auxiliary-reduction and his global rule of comparative-simplification, which are repeated here as (35) and (36).

(35)   If, at any point in the syntax, a constituent immediately following *be* is deleted, then, later in the phonology, that *be* cannot undergo stress-lowering (and subsequent contraction). [91: 632]

(36)   With *earlier than,* the rule of comparative simplification can apply only if the verb modified by *at a time* is identical to the verb originally modified by *at which.* [91: 635]

It will be recalled that (35) is the global rule which is proposed to account for the difference between (37a) and (37b).

(37) a.   Sam's on the job in the mornings and Harry is _____ in the afternoons.
     b.   *Sam's on the job in the mornings and Harry's _____ in the afternoons.

The second rule, (36), is the global rule which allows for (38), while prohibiting others; cf. [8] for criticism.

(38)   John left *at a time which was* earlier than *the time at which* Bill left $\Longrightarrow$
      John left _____ earlier than _____ Bill left.

Now the two global rules proposed by Lakoff are incompatible in view of the following observations.

(39) The concert is *at a time which is* earlier than *the time at which* the play is $\Longrightarrow$
The concert is _____ earlier than _____ the play.

Notice that (39) is provided for by global rule (36), whereas global rule (35) predicts, as a consequence, that (40) is ungrammatical.

(40) The concert's earlier than the play.

In view of this false prediction, it would be an error to conclude that global rules are sterile. They have, on the contrary, in their relatively short gestation, already given birth to contradictions.

NOTES TO CHAPTER 3

[1]This immunization trait of generative semantics is made particularly obvious by the repeated use of phrases such as "virtually synonymous," "essential paraphrase," and the like. Until and unless *virtual synonymy, essential paraphrase,* etc., are made explicit, they can only be taken as contentless dodges.

[2]For example, generative semantics can stipulate that (8a) not apply unless (8b) has already applied, in which case ŋawuŋawu is not affected at all, although words with nonapical consonants in word-final position underlyingly will be.

[3]That is, by linear ordering. Incidentally, I am assuming that the definition of linear ordering within the standard theory includes an asymmetry condition: If A precedes B, then B does not precede A. Irreflexivity follows trivially from this condition and *modus ponens* when A and B are taken to be the same rule. However, recent research indicates that under certain conditions rules can be reflexive. Even within these approaches, however, as, for example, the approach of Phelps [120] and the references cited there, (10) is not a possible derivation.

[4]Generative semantics often invokes *natural logic* in addition to global rules. For example, Emonds writes,

> Lakoff . . . apparently feels that any syntactic analysis which uses categories that do not appear in NATURAL LOGIC is *a priori* unacceptable. He returns to this theme in discussing Baker and Brame's alternative to an analysis given by Geis (ms) of certain comparatives which requires a global constraint. Their analysis . . . "uses categories AP and DEG, which as usual have no external motivation." Lakoff refuses to consider the merits of their analysis, which employs categories which are well-motivated internal to lan-

guage (syntactically). This refusal seems to me like requiring that philosophy define *a priori* the notions of science, in which case we would never have gotten to gravity, relativity, etc. [57: 56]

[5] For some discussion of these issues as they relate to the cycle, see [15].

[6] Actually, Lakoff [93] characterizes yet a third proposal of [8] as an ad hoc "coding mechanism." This proposal concerns examples such as the following:

(i)   John and someone were dancing, but I don't know who.
(ii)   John didn't lift a finger to help, but Bill did.

Lakoff remarks: "I, like Baker and Brame, find both (i) and (ii) fully grammatical . . . " [93: 82]. For the record, Brame finds (i) and (ii) totally ungrammatical. Moreover, Baker and Brame explicitly state concerning judgments vis-à-vis (i) and (ii): "we feel that the judgments about the relevant sentences are anything but secure . . . " [8: 62] and note in connection with (i) that "many speakers find it completely ungrammatical" [8: 61]. Baker and Brame also pointed out that the original source of (i)—Ross [140]—attributes a double question mark to it, whereas Lakoff in [91] fails to mention Ross's judgment, instead attributing full grammaticality to the example on behalf of Ross. This manipulation of the data is perhaps illustrative of the care with which Lakoff has read the response to his original article on global rules.

[7] In fact, this point is made by Perry in [116].

EPILOGUE TO PART I
A FINAL VERDICT

In chapters 1–3 a number of recent proposals of generative semantics have been discussed and criticized. Some of the charges directed against this approach to the study of natural language include the following:

1. Generative semantics is not sufficiently explicit (no rules, no explicit underlying structures, no formalization of global rules, no characterization of semantic predicates) to provide an unambiguous basis for comparison with current explicit theories, such as the standard theory. Cf. chapter 1.
2. Generative semantics is a breeding ground for syntactic irregularity as a consequence of its exception devices, unnaturally remote underlying representations, its abolition of deep structure and incorporation of semantic predicates and global devices, and its blurring of the distinction between the lexicon and transformations as well as between syntax and semantics. Cf. chapter 2.
3. Generative semantics is prescientific and irrefutable as a consequence, in part, of its incorporation of semantic predicates and global mechanisms. Cf. chapter 3.
4. Generative semantics is antiabstractionist inasmuch as it refuses to stray from what it alleges to be the phonetic or semantic given. Structures not directly mirroring one or the other are rejected. Cf. chapter 1, note 1.
5. Generative semantics gives up the quest for universals as a consequence of its adoption of global rules (and its abolition of ordering, etc.). Cf. chapter 3.

In addition to these points, I think it can be accurately said that generative semantics fails on almost every single proposal or suggestion for the analysis of a fragment of English grammar that it has advanced. To mention just a sample of the refutational literature documenting this assertion, I will cite the responses of Chomsky [40], Culicover [48], and

Schachter [146] to Lakoff's claim [86] that adjectives are verbs, to Ross's arguments [139] for treating adjectives as noun phrases, and to Bach's proposals [5] concerning nouns as predicates; the responses of Chomsky [43], and Jackendoff [74] to the proposals of Carden [28], [29] and Lakoff [92] for treating quantifiers as underlying predicates; Bresnan's critique [22] of the Ross-Perlmutter abstract source for comparatives [143]; Berman's arguments [11] against McCawley's VSO analysis [105] of English; the responses of Fodor [61] and Ruwet [144] to the approach of Lakoff [87] and McCawley [103] to causatives; the rebuttals of Bowers [13], Kimball [82], Leben [97], Ronat [133], and Ruwet [144] to Postal's analysis of *remind* [124]; Ruwet's response [144] to Postal's psych predicates [126]; the critiques by Bresnan [17] and Chomsky [43] of Lakoff's treatment [88] of instrumental adverbs as verbs; the responses of Anderson [2], Fraser [64], and Hasegawa [69] to Ross's performative analysis [141]; the rebuttals of Emonds [57] and Milsark [109] to Ross's global rule [142] and Postal's global approach to pronominalization [127]; Quicoli's attack [131] on Lakoff's global treatment of Greek [91]; Selkirk's demonstration [150] of the poverty of Lakoff's global treatment [91] of contraction and reduction in English; the Baker-Brame response [8] to Lakoff's global proposals [91]; Hust's discussion [71] of Lakoff's analysis of *dissuade* [89], [92]; and so on.

Works such as these do tend to support the verdict delivered here and provide us with additional articles of criticism:

6. The gross underlying deformations proposed by generative semantics leave unexplained the high degree of convergence of many of these structures at the level of surface structure.
7. Many of the transformations proposed within the generative semantics framework evidently violate independently motivated syntactic constraints.
8. Lexical decomposition leaves unexplained many distributional similarities and differences, e.g., the similarities between *persuade* and *persuade not* and the differences between *dissuade* and *persuade not*. Cf. [71] and section 1.1.4.
9. In view of the generative semanticists' claim that most parts of speech are underlying predicates, it is unclear that the obvious differences between nouns, verbs, adjectives, etc., can be accounted for.[1]

In the face of this indictment, it is not surprising that generative semanticists should propose ever more far-fetched devices such as "transderiva-tional constraints" (due to Perlmutter, Hankamer, et al., cf. [68]).[2]

NOTES TO EPILOGUE

[1]Ross [139: 353] accepts "the correctness of the claim that adjectives and verbs are members of the same lexical category," but continues, "It should be obvious, however, that to accept this claim is not to maintain that verbs and adjectives behave identically in all respects, but only that their deep similarities outweigh their superficial differences . . . " Contrast these remarks with Culicover's: "To say that the identical categorization of two previously distinct categories explains why it is that they share certain properties avoids the question of why it is that they do not share all properties; in fact, it explains nothing at all" [48: 15].

[2]One cannot help but wonder what will happen when such proposals are no longer taken seriously. My original speculation was that generative semanticists would sponsor a "new theory" which would thereby enable them to write off their earlier proposals as old hat, in view of the "new theory." This prediction now appears to be borne out with respect to Perlmutter, Postal, and McCawley, who have apparently embraced "relational grammar." Of course, it is perfectly ra-tional to come up with a new theory when an old one has defects, but one wonders how it was possible to argue so vehemently for a bad theory, as in [124], in the face of so much counterevidence.

Part II   The Standard Theory

Chapter 4

The VP Controversy

Having discussed and criticized generative semantics in the foregoing pages, I now wish to concentrate on the (extended) standard theory of transformational grammar and point to what I consider to be some of its soft spots. In this chapter, the recent controversy between Berman and Szamosi and Bresnan will be reviewed and the issues delineated.[1] This chapter sets the scene for what follows in chapter 5, where Equi-NP Deletion is investigated and rejected and where some, perhaps disturbing consequences are drawn. It is the goal of chapter 6, the final chapter, to provide viable alternatives to the standard theory.

4.1 BRESNAN'S VP HYPOTHESIS

Postal [126], among others, has assumed that sentences such as (1a) [126:(3.3)] derive from more abstract structures similar to (1b) by a rule shifting the object of the embedded S into the subject position of the matrix S.[2]

(1) a. Jack was difficult for Tony to hit.
     b. It was difficult [for Tony to hit Jack]$_S$

Bresnan [19] has provided us with important new arguments showing that the complement underlying (1a) is not in fact an S complement, but rather a PP + VP complement. Thus, within Bresnan's framework (1a) derives not from (1b), but from (2a), and (2b) derives not from (2c), but rather from (2d).

(2) a. It was difficult [for Tony]$_{PP}$ [to hit Jack]$_{VP}$
     b. It will be tough for at least some students to be in class on time.
     c. It will be tough [for at least some students to be in class on time]$_S$
     d. It will be tough [for at least some students]$_{PP}$ [to be in class on time]$_{VP}$

73

Bresnan's arguments will be summarized in this section. First, she notes that if there were an S complement in (2b) in deep structure, the rule of *there*-Insertion would be expected to be applicable. But, according to Bresnan, the result is ungrammatical.[3]

(3) *It will be tough for there to be at least some students in class on time.

By contrast, sentences with true S complements do exhibit *there*-Insertion, as shown by Bresnan's [19: (21)], repeated here as (4a, b).

(4) a. The administration is eager for there to be at least some students in class on time.
     b. It wouldn't surprise me for there to be countless revolutionaries among the secretaries.

Second, Bresnan notes that "the *for*-complement of a true sentential complement allows many types of objects which the preposition *for* after *tough* does not"; [19: (22)]:

(5) a. *It was tough for that theorem on modules to become known.
     b. Emmy was eager for that theorem on modules to become known.
     c. *It would be tough for a book on Hittite to please John.
     d. It would surprise me for a book on Hittite to please John.

As a third argument for VP, Bresnan notes that sentences bearing true S complements alternate in allowing the complement to be shifted by a rule of S-Shift; [19: (23)]:

(6) a. It is surprising [for a woman to act that way]$_S$
     b. [For a woman to act that way]$_S$ is surprising

Predicates such as *tough* do not confirm this distribution of S; [19: (24)]:

(7) a. It's tough for students to grasp this concept.
     b. *For students to grasp this concept is tough.

All of the facts adduced by Bresnan follow as a natural consequence of her VP hypothesis: Object-Shift predicates select VP complements and the rule of Object-Shift is formulated so as to apply to VP complements. *There*-Insertion, which applies to S's, will not be applicable, explaining why (3) is ungrammatical. S-Shift will not be applicable, explaining why (7b) is ungrammatical. And the PP of (2) is not in the deep subject position of the embedded S, but rather is a complement to the matrix verb, thus explaining why there are restrictions on the object of *for*. Since these facts follow from Bresnan's analysis without ad hoc theoretical elaboration, we must recognize that her analysis provides an explanation for the range of phenomena that are at best only *described* within a framework such as that of Postal [126]. Moreover, as Bresnan points out, her analysis makes a prediction: since Object-Shift is formulated so as to apply to VP complements, the prediction is that objects cannot shift from true S complements. This prediction is borne out by the following sentences provided by Postal [126: 13.22 and p. 113, fn. 9]:

(8) a. *You are tough for me to believe that Harry hates.
     b. *Harriet is tough for me to stop Bill's looking at.

Bresnan thus explains the ungrammaticality of (8), for such strings cannot arise within her framework. This fact constitutes a fourth argument for the VP status of Object-Shift predicates.

The latter argument is particularly powerful. Taken in conjunction with certain facts about subcategorization, it provides a beautiful explanation for an otherwise intractable set of data. Consider the fact that subcategorization is a lexical property; cf. Chomsky [36]. For example, predicates may select a wide range of complements. Thus, *pinch* selects only an NP complement, whereas *know* selects NP and S, in addition to others. Given that predicates select such major categories as NP, S, and AP, we should expect to find that some predicates such as *tough* select the major category VP. This gap is indeed filled in Bresnan's framework. Further, we might expect to find some predicates that select both S and VP. As noted by Bresnan, Lees [99] adduced evidence confirming the existence of such predicates. Thus, *good* selects either VP or S, as suggested by the ambiguity of sentences such as *it is good for John to leave*, which may be analyzed as *it is good [for John to leave]*$_S$ or as *it is good [for John]*$_{PP}$ *[to leave]*$_{VP}$.

In light of the preceding, consider the following examples:

(9) a. It is not good for Communists to be involved in defense plants.

b. It is not good for there to be Communists involved in defense plants.

c. Defense plants are not good for Communists to be involved in.

As noted by Lees, sentences such as (9a) are ambiguous between an S and PP + VP interpretation (corresponding to right and left wing interpretations respectively in these nice examples brought to my attention by Joe Emonds). Since *there*-Insertion applies only to S structures, there is an explanation for why (9b) is unambiguous, bearing only the S interpretation of (9a). If Bresnan is correct in formulating Object-Shift so as to apply to VP complements, and not to S complements, then (9c) should also be unambiguous, bearing only the VP interpretation of (9a). This prediction is borne out. In addition Bresnan predicts that Object-Shift cannot apply to (9b), and again, her prediction is borne out as proved by (10).

(10)   *Defense plants are not good for there to be Communists involved in.

To quote Bresnan, "While Postal's version states that Object Shift may not occur across *more than one* S-bracket, the version of the rule given here states, in effect, that Object Shift may not occur across *any* S-brackets." She continues, "there is therefore an empirical difference between these two versions," and notes that the "crucial evidence" is provided by examples like (9) and (10). She remarks that "the evidence . . . crucially favors an 'intra-sentence' version of the rule over any 'cross-sentence' version," noting that "any version like Postal's will incorrectly predict that 26a [similar to (10)] is a grammatical sentence."

Bresnan offers a further argument in support of her VP hypothesis. She notes that incorrect stress would be generated if there were an S associated with Object-Shift predicates. The argument is based on her Ordering Hypothesis, which is the principle topic of her 1971 paper, and will not be repeated here.

I have summarized Bresnan's arguments for the VP hypothesis because their importance has been missed by her critics. It should perhaps be reemphasized that the following facts *follow* from the VP hypothesis:

(11)   i.   There is no *there*-Insertion when VP is selected.
       ii. There are lexical restrictions on PP when PP + VP is selected.
       iii. There is no S-Shift when VP is selected.

iv. There is no Object-Shift when S is selected.
v. Subcategorization of some Object-Shift predicates for VP fills a gap.
vi. Correct stress is predicted when VP is selected.

Those who would persist in retaining the S structure for Object-Shift predicate complements must do as well in answering the following questions:

(12)   i.   Why does *there*-Insertion not apply in general to Object-Shift predicates?

      ii.   Why are there restrictions on PP of Object-Shift predicates?

      iii.   Why does S-Shift not in general apply to Object-Shift complements?

      iv.   Why does Object-Shift not in general apply to S complements of Object-Shift predicates?

      v.   Why do some Object-Shift predicates not select VP complements?

      vi.   How is stress assigned to sentences bearing Object-Shift predicates?

Bresnan answers all six questions with one powerful hypothesis—what I have referred to in the preceding as the VP hypothesis. Let us turn now to the criticism leveled against Bresnan by Berman and Szamosi [12] and ask how the latter answer the questions posed in (12).

4.2 BERMAN AND SZAMOSI ON OBJECT-SHIFT

In discussing Bresnan's VP hypothesis, Berman and Szamosi remark, "as it turns out, the S-structure is much closer to the mark in all respects." I will now summarize their response, show that their remark is false, and demonstrate that their S-comp structure requires ad hoc theoretical elaboration of a sort which further vitiates their analysis.

First, Berman and Szamosi note that there are Object-Shift predicates that allow two instances of *for NP;* their [12: (77a, b)] are repeated here as (13a, b):

(13)   a.   For his wife to accept this view would be tough for John.

      b.   It would be tough for John for his wife to accept this view.

Second, they note that there are Object-Shift predicates that do allow *there*-Insertion [12: (79) and (80)]:

(14) a. It's impossible for there to be five mistakes in that paper.
　　 b. It's a bitch for there to be so many papers to grade.

Third, there are restrictions on PP of Object-Shift predicates because there is a PP in the matrix S in addition to an embedded complement S, but the matrix PP is usually optional [12: (84)]:

(15) It's impossible for that theorem on modules to become known (if you don't publish it).

Fourth, there are Object-Shift predicates that do allow S-Shift.

(16) a. It is impossible for Sam to dislike Mary.
　　 b. For Sam to dislike Mary is impossible. [12: fn. 22]

Fifth, Object-Shift does not move objects across S-boundaries because of "the structural description of the rule."

Finally, Berman and Szamosi reject Bresnan's ordering hypothesis and concomitant explanation for sentential stress of complex sentences in English.

It is evident that Berman and Szamosi's answers to the questions posed in (12) are essentially the following:

(17) i. *there*-Insertion does apply to Object-Shift predicate complements.
　 ii. There are restrictions on PP because there are PP + S complements.
　 iii. S-Shift does apply to Object-Shift predicate complements.
　 iv. Object-Shift does not apply across S-boundaries because of the formal statement of Object-Shift.
　 v. ?
　 vi. Bresnan's ordering hypothesis is "completely untenable" because it does not predict all possible sentential stress.

I will now indicate why the response of Berman and Szamosi is irrelevant to the VP hypothesis advanced by Bresnan. Let us consider *there-*

Insertion, S-Shift, and Berman and Szamosi's remarks concerning (13). Berman and Szamosi make it appear as though the existence of (14) and (16) refutes Bresnan's VP hypothesis. Even a cursory reading of Bresnan's original paper, however, reveals that she is aware of such examples. She notes that subcategorization is a lexical property, that some Object-Shift predicates are expected to be subcategorized so as to select both VP and S complements, and that speakers will differ to some extent in respect to which predicates select both VP and S complements. To document this assertion, I cite Bresnan's remarks to the effect that "there is in fact a class of adjectives permitting both S and PP + VP complements—namely, the class including *good, bad, sweet, pleasant,* and *appropriate*." In fact, a relevant sentence exhibiting *there*-Insertion has already been given in (9). Bresnan further notes that "Lees maintains a clear distinction between the ambiguous class (*good;* his type 7) and the unambiguous class (*hard, tough;* his type 8)" and discerningly observes that "some speakers may class certain of the latter with the former, permitting sentences like this: *For John to please Mary is* {*hard, easy, difficult*}." Bresnan recognizes Postal as one such speaker. Thus, she is well aware that some speakers allow a wider subcategorization for some Object-Shift predicates. This, however, is a fact about subcategorization and is not germane to the issue of the existence of VP complements. Just because some Object-Shift complements select S, in addition to VP, this in no sense implies that the VP complements are S complements in underlying representations. Berman and Szamosi's reasoning is not new to the field. It goes something like this: Because some verbs take S complements, all complements to those verbs must be S complements. By parity of reasoning we could conclude that the NP direct object complement of *expect* in *John expected Mary* is really an S since we do find S complements to *expect,* as in *John expected that Mary would come.* Such reasoning, like that adopted by Berman and Szamosi, is obviously unacceptable. A real argument would necessarily show that NP patterns like S in a wide range of contexts or that postulation of S leads to an explanation for otherwise puzzling phenomena. No such argument appears likely. Similarly, for Berman and Szamosi to prove that *to please John* in *it is tough to please John* derives from an underlying S, they would have to show that VP patterns like S or that by postulating S, other problems are resolved as a consequence. They offer no such evidence. Consequently, their facts concerning *there*-Insertion and S-Shift are irrelevant. On similar grounds, (13) is irrelevant to the issue of the VP hypothesis. In fact, once again Bresnan herself quite explicitly notes that some Object-Shift predicates permit two *for*-NP phrases and cites the following example:

(18)   It would be good for Mary for her to learn karate.

But Bresnan remarks that such examples display "the possibility PP + S" in their lexical subcategorization.

As for Berman and Szamosi's response to (12ii), they essentially accept Bresnan's argument that PP is not part of the complement S (contra Postal [126]), but they attempt to preserve the S structure by requiring Equi-NP Deletion to operate, eliminating the putative underlying subject of the embedded complement. I shall return below to a criticism of the unmotivated devices this assumption entails.

Turning now to (17iv), that is, to Berman and Szamosi's account of the ungrammaticality of (8) and (10), we note that their claim that such facts "bear only on the structural description of the rule, and not on the underlying structures of sentences containing predicates like *tough*, as Bresnan claims," is considerably weakened by the fact that Berman and Szamosi offer no formulation of their structural description so as to provide a basis for comparison. Moreover, they are mistaken in assuming that the relevant facts are unrelated to the underlying structures of the crucial sentences. Motivation of underlying structures and syntactic rules go hand in hand and there is little to be gained by advancing a priori arguments to the effect that the ungrammaticality of (8) and (10) has nothing to do with underlying representations. Berman and Szamosi's mode of reasoning is again well known in the field. It assumes that transformational devices are to be favored over structural devices in accounting for ungrammaticality. We shall return to this point below, but we find it somewhat revealing that in the one work in which an explicit structural description is provided, in Berman [10], the embedded S complement is 'preserved' by a bare S bracket.[4]

(19) $[_S[_{NP}[_S$V   X   NP   Y]] Adj   for NP]

Notice that in this formulation of the structural description of Object-Shift, the bare S brackets ensure the absence of the subject. It is curious that S must be included for the sole reason that the abstract S was postulated in underlying representations. In Berman [10] a subject-crossing constraint is mentioned, and evidently this constraint is intended to provide an independent account of the ungrammaticality of (8) and (10). It should be noted that no such constraint is required in Bresnan's framework.[5]

Berman and Szamosi provide no answer to (12v), but perhaps this is because the argument is implicit in Bresnan [19]. Turning to (12vi), and Berman and Szamosi's response, recorded as (17vi), we observe that not only do they misinterpret Bresnan's ordering hypothesis, but that they do not provide an alternative to her account of a wide range of heretofore unexplained stress contours. Bresnan [23] gives a detailed defense against Berman and Szamosi's critique of this point.

Let us now return to *there*-Insertion and S-Shift and related matters. As noted above, sentences such as (14) and (16), and (13), are irrelevant to the basic issue, being instead evidence for multiple subcategorization as argued explicitly by Bresnan. The real test of Berman and Szamosi's analysis devolves on its account of the ungrammaticality of Bresnan's examples (3), (7b), and (10), which are repeated here as (20):

(20) a. *It will be tough for there to be at least some students in class on time.
      b. *For students to grasp this concept is tough.
      c. *Such things are not good for there to be children involved in.

In addition Berman and Szamosi must account for the ungrammaticality of examples such as the following [12: fn. 4]:

(21) *It would be tough for John for him to accept this view.

Let us consider (21) first. In Berman and Szamosi we read that such examples are ruled out by "making Equi-NP Deletion obligatory, or the like." As for (20a), these authors suggest that "one possibility is subcategorizing some, but not all Tough-movement predicates for an obligatory prepositional phrase." They continue, "recall that, for many Tough-movement predicates, Equi-NP Deletion (or something equivalent) of an embedded subject coreferential to the matrix prepositional phrase is obligatory." Thus, Berman and Szamosi account for (21) and (20a) by subcategorizing *tough* for PP + S and by marking *tough* to obligatorily undergo Equi-NP Deletion. The ad hoc nature of this account cannot be glossed over with words such as "or the like" or "or something equivalent," for essentially the effect of marking *tough* to obligatorily undergo Equi-NP Deletion, followed by pruning of the S node, is just to ensure that *tough* ends up with a PP + VP complement, which is what Bresnan accomplishes straightaway. Thus, in "preserving" the S structure of the complement to *tough,* Berman and Szamosi require a new ad hoc restriction of obligatory rule application (in addition to a rule of pruning). It is important to recognize that this is an additional restriction. Both Bresnan and Berman and Szamosi mark *tough* for subcategorizational restrictions, PP + VP in the case of Bresnan, and PP + S in the case of Berman and Szamosi. But it is only the latter who require the new obligatory application of Equi-NP Deletion for predicates such as *tough.* The extra rule-governing feature is unneeded in Bresnan's approach, a significant argument for her VP hypothesis.[6]

There is a further difficulty that emerges from Berman and Szamosi's account of (20a) as a result of their requirement that a matrix PP be obligatory. Sentences such as (22a) [12: fn. 21] derive from (22b).

(22) a. It's tough to talk to idiots.
      b. It's tough [for PRO]$_{PP}$ [PRO talk to idiots]$_S$

It is somewhat surprising that preservation of the S-structure requires such an elaboration of abstract structure which just happens to result in the surface VP-structure with which Bresnan commences. The implausibility of abstract structures such as (22b) is further revealed by an additional constraint it entails within the Berman and Szamosi framework. Berman and Szamosi note that they should expect the following derivation [12: fn. 21]:

(23) a. It would be tough [for PRO]$_{PP}$ [for Nixon to be President again]$_S$ $\Longrightarrow$
      b. It would be tough for Nixon to be President again.

But Berman and Szamosi observe that (23b) has but a single reading in which *Nixon* is within the matrix clause. To block the derivation in (23), they note that "an additional constraint would be needed, to the effect that if the matrix prepositional phrase contains PRO, Equi must apply; and derivations in which it cannot apply, because there is no coreference, are blocked." Notice that the constraint here is not that if the embedded subject is identical to the matrix object of the preposition, Equi is obligatory, as above, but rather that the embedded subject must necessarily be identical to the matrix object of the preposition if that object is PRO. Such a new constraint is of course a consequence of "preserving" the S-structure and by Berman and Szamosi's admission, "such a constraint is admittedly strange . . . " As so often happens, more and more abstract underlying structures raise more questions than they answer. Again the constraint on identity of embedded subject and matrix object of the preposition, like the constraint on obligatory Equi-NP Deletion, is designed so as to ensure that we end up with a surface VP, which is what Bresnan assumes from the beginning.

Returning to (20) we see that (20b) is blocked by Berman and Szamosi by subcategorizing *tough* "for an obligatory prepositional phrase." This is of course the requirement that leads to the two ad hoc restrictions noted directly above. Moving on to (20c), we have already noted that Berman and Szamosi would formulate Object-Shift with a bare subjectless S and that (19) represents the structural description of this rule as given in Berman's [10]. We must ask, however, if (19) satisfactorily prohibits objects from moving out of sentences with subjects. The answer is obviously no, as noted by Berman herself, since the NP flanked by X and Y in (19) can be embedded in an S which is itself embedded in the innermost S of (19). Thus, in fn. 8 to Berman's [10], we find the following:

(24)   a.   It is impossible to believe that John stole that book.
       b.   *That book is impossible to believe that John stole.

To block (24b) Berman proposes yet another constraint: "There is an additional restriction on Tough-movement which blocks movement out of tensed clauses . . . " Again it should be noted that the ungrammaticality of (24) follows from Bresnan's analysis, which requires no extra constraint.[7]

4.3   CONCLUSION

The theoretical mechanisms required by Berman and Szamosi are summarized as (25):

(25)   i.   Obligatory subcategorization of Object-Shift predicates such as *tough*.
       ii.   Obligatory Equi-NP Deletion for predicates such as *tough*.
       iii. Obligatory coreference for PRO in predicates such as *tough*.
       iv.   Rule pruning S.
       v.   Formulation of Object-Shift with bare S brackets.

vi. Subject-crossing constraint.

vii. Constraint prohibiting Object-Shift from applying to tensed sentences.

Notice that (25i–iv) all have the same effect of bringing about a VP structure. This fact represents a deeper loss of generalization, for, within the Berman and Szamosi framework, it is completely accidental that these four constraints have the same effect. Now there are, no doubt, those who will see in this a deep, mysterious conspiracy. But this is only to suggest that something has been missed. In this case, the fact that we end up with a VP follows as an automatic consequence of Bresnan's VP hypothesis. It is also to be noted that (25v–vii) are designed to prevent bad consequences from resulting in the case of true sentential complements. Such ad hoc accretions are required only because the distinction between VP and S is blurred in the first place, as when Berman and Szamosi derive their VP's from S's. The proliferation of constraints in (25) suggests that something is indeed missed by Berman and Szamosi. Bresnan's arguments are not to be lightly cast aside. They can be interpreted as providing support for the category VP, a category recently abandoned by generative semanticists. [8]

NOTES TO CHAPTER 4

[1] This chapter is a revised version of an article which appeared in *Linguistic Analysis* 1, 191–203.

[2] Cf. also [130]. Actually Postal assumes that (1b) derives from the more abstract (i) by Extraposition before undergoing shift of the complement object.

(i) It [for Tony to hit Jack]$_S$ was difficult.

Still later in his development, Postal opts for an analysis including Psych-Movement. Arguments against (1b) are a fortiori arguments against (i) and the Psych-Movement analysis, so that such details need not detain us here.

Postal's choice of "*Tough*-movement" as the name for the object-shifting transformation is unfortunate inasmuch as some speakers do not admit *tough* in the class of Object-Shift predicates. There is, moreover, little reason to focus on a specific member of this class. Therefore, the "Object-Shift" terminology of Bresnan will be employed in the sequel.

[3] I agree with Bresnan's judgments, as do Berman and Szamosi. However, there will be those who insist that (3) is grammatical. In view of the possibility of

multiple subcategorization of some Object-Shift predicates (cf. infra), it would not be surprising to find some speakers who subcategorize *tough* for S complements in addition to VP complements. If this is the case, however, such speakers should also accept (7b) of the main text. Those who do not accept (7b), yet claim to accept (3), may, after all, be confusing *tough* with Object-Shift predicates that do admit multiple subcategorization.

[4]Concerning the formation of Object-Shift, Berman remarks: "The actual mechanics of the rule remain mysterious" [10: 37]. As this discussion indicates, rules will continue to remain mysterious, and issues clouded, in the absence of explicit analyses.

[5]It is surprising that Berman [10] fails to credit Chomsky [44] for the Specified Subject and Tensed S Conditions. (Although both Chomsky's and Berman's papers were published in 1973, Chomsky's was available and widely disseminated in 1970.) However, these conditions do not provide support for the abstract S analysis since they are questionable, cf. [16].

[6]Berman and Szamosi claim that there are dialects of English in which the following judgments hold:

(a)   It would be tough for John for his wife to accept this view.
(b)   *It would be tough for John for him to accept this view.

They point out that such facts would require Bresnan to adopt a special constraint to rule out (b), while allowing (a), and conclude from this that their S-structure, with concomitant obligatory Equi-NP Deletion, is somehow to be preferred. I fail to understand the reasoning involved, since if such dialects do in fact exist, then both Berman and Szamosi and Bresnan require additional ad hoc mechanisms: the former require obligatory Equi-NP Deletion and the latter, obligatory noncoreference. It would thus be a standoff; there would be no argument either way. For dialects such as Bresnan's, which I believe reject both (a) and (b), there is, however, an argument for Bresnan's analysis. Thus, the existence of (a) and (b) would only cancel out this argument for that dialect; it would not support Berman and Szamosi. Incidentally, I am sceptical about the grammaticality judgments displayed in (a) and (b) and feel that much more caution could be exercised in dialect arguments.

[7]See fn. 5 concerning Chomsky's Tensed S Condition.

[8]Lasnik and Fiengo [96] have recently argued that the complement object of Object-Shift predicates originates in the matrix subject position. Thus, in place of a rule of Object-Shift, they propose a rule of Object-Deletion. Their insight concerning the origin of the relevant NP is shown to follow from more general considerations below. However, I differ in assuming that there is no complement

object in base structures and I do not invoke Chomsky's Specified Subject and Tensed S Conditions. Thus, I claim there is an interpretive rule shifting the subject of Object-Shift predicates into the complement VP object position, or else placing a copy of it there. For additional remarks on the Berman and Szamosi analysis, see the article by Lasnik and Fiengo. For some criticism of the latter, see Ioup [72].

Chapter 5

Equi-NP Deletion Revisited

5.1 INTRODUCTION: EQUI-NP DELETION AND IDENTITY

One of the few transformational rules which has not been subjected to a critical reevaluation is the rule which has come to be known as Equi-NP Deletion. A recent description of this rule is given by McCawley in [105].

> There is a transformation, called Equi-NP Deletion, which deletes the first noun phrase of an embedded clause if it matches a certain NP of the clause containing it, as in *Max wants to drink a daiquiri,* where the subject of *drink* has been deleted under identity with the subject of *want*.

McCawley proposes the following derivation of the example he cites:

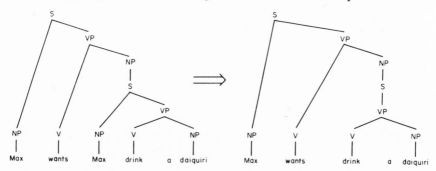

Such derivations are characteristic of an approach which can be ascribed to the standard theory of transformational syntax; cf. [36]. This approach incorporates a rule which deletes a fully specified NP under identity with another NP, which, following Postal, I will refer to as the controller. Since the appearance of [98: 75–76], deletion under identity has subsumed more than just *string identity;* it has incorporated the more restrictive *structural identity.* In the present context, deletion under identity requires not only that the two instances of the string *Max* be identical in the example cited above, but also that the structure associated with the two NP's dominating these strings be identical. It is obvious that structural identity implies (terminal) string identity, but the converse is false.

It is customary to further constrain Equi-NP Deletion in order to account for the difference between the following examples:

(1) Max wants to drink a daiquiri.
(2) Max wants Max to drink a daiquiri.

Both (1) and (2) are well-formed sentences of English. Yet (1) and (2) would both result in (1) if McCawley's structures were adopted without refinement. Evidently, (1) and (2) differ in that the two occurrences of *Max* in (2) do not refer to the same individual, whereas the deleted instance of *Max* and its controller do indeed refer to the same individual in McCawley's derivation of (1). It is therefore said that Equi-NP Deletion applies only to coreferential NP's, and, traditionally, coreferentiality is represented in the standard theory by indices; cf. [36: 146].

Following Chomsky [36: 146], I will denote structural identity together with coreferentiality (where relevant) by the term *strict identity*. Indices are, for Chomsky, features, and thus identity of indices falls under his conception of structural identity.[1]

Strict identity is therefore a condition on the application of Equi-NP Deletion within the standard framework. It should be emphasized, however, that many linguists have not assumed this condition to be ad hoc to Equi-NP Deletion. Chomsky, for example, as early as 1964, enounced a general hypothesis which has come to be known as the principle of *unique recoverability of deletion*:

> . . . an erasure transformation can use a term X of its proper analysis to erase a term Y of the proper analysis only if X and Y are identical [36: 177]

"Identity" in this quote is intended to incorporate structural identity, and, hence, coreferentiality in the particular case of Equi-NP Deletion.[2] Thus, an NP which is not strictly identical to its would be controller would not be uniquely recoverable if deleted by Equi-NP Deletion, since the information for unique recoverability would not be present in the structure resulting from its application. By contrast, NP's which are coreferential with, and structurally identical to, their controllers are deletable, and the controller presumably constitutes the information relevant to unique re-

88

coverability. In view of these observations, the principle of unique re-coverability of deletion is often formulated as follows:[3]

(3)   Deletion transformations apply just in case the deleted terms are uniquely recoverable.

In what follows I will seek to provide an explanation for a range of data which the standard theory incorporating Equi-NP Deletion describes. The conclusion I will draw—that there is no rule of Equi-NP Deletion—will have consequences for the correct formulation of a class of movement rules of the standard theory and will bear on the recent transformational dichotomy of root and structure-preserving transformations of [54] and [58].

5.2   CONTRA EQUI-NP DELETION

The problems which the standard theory must confront as a consequence of Equi-NP Deletion are more difficult than generally recognized. Take, for example, the generally accepted cyclic rule of *there*-Insertion, which is postulated to relate sentences such as the following:

(4)   a.   A few students were in class on time.
      b.   There were a few students in class on time.

Consider the claim that (5b) derives from (5a) via Equi-NP Deletion.

(5)   a.   A few students$_i$ tried [for a few students$_i$ to be in class on time]$_{S_1}$
      b.   A few students tried to be in class on time.

The next sentence illustrates that *there*-Insertion is applicable to embedded infinitive phrases:

(6)   John would like for there to be a few students in class on time.

It should be possible, however, to apply *there*-Insertion on the S_1 cycle of (5a) since it is a cyclic rule.

(7)   *A few students tried for there to be a few students in class on time.

The fact is that such an application of *there*-Insertion yields the ungrammatical (7), to which Equi-NP Deletion is inapplicable. This problem also arises for predicates such as *want*, where we are left with NP's which are marked as coreferential but cannot be so interpreted, as in

(8) a. A few students$_i$ want [for a few students$_i$ to be in class on time]$_{S_1}$
     b. *A few students$_i$ want there to be a few students$_i$ in class on time.

If there were a rule of Equi-NP Deletion, giving rise to (5b) from (5a), we would expect (7) to be acceptable. Since it is not, we may conclude that Equi-NP Deletion is not in fact a rule.[4]

To salvage Equi-NP Deletion, it is necessary to adopt an ad hoc constraint along the lines of (9).

(9) *there*-Insertion must not apply to coreferential NP's.

Alternatively, *there*-Insertion itself might be abandoned as has been argued independently in [77].

The root of the problem does not reside in *there*-Insertion, however. In [51] Dougherty formulates a rule of Quantifier-Postposition to relate the following pairs [51: (256a,b), (257a, b), (258a, b)]:

(10) a. Each of the men will drink a beer.
      b. The men each will drink a beer.

(11) a. Both of the men will drink a beer.
      b. The men both will drink a beer.

(12) a. All of the men will drink a beer.
      b. The men all will drink a beer.

Dougherty formulates Quantifier-Postposition as follows:

(13) SD: $(_S(_{NP} \underset{[-dis]}{Q}\ M_1)(_{VP}M_2))$

      SC: $(_S(_{NP}M_1)(_{VP}\underset{[-dis]}{Q}\ M_2))$

where $\underset{[-dis]}{Q}$ = *each, all, both;* M = variable

If this formulation of Quantifier-Postposition is correct and if there is a rule of Raising which shifts the subject of embedded complements into the object position of the matrix S with predicates such as *expect,* then the following sentences would prove that Quantifier-Postposition is cyclic:

(14) a. We expect each of the men to drink a beer.
      b. We expect the men each to drink a beer.

In order to derive (14b) from (14a) using (13), it would be necessary to apply Quantifier-Postposition before the subject of the complement is extracted by Raising since (13) applies only to subjects.

The implications of Quantifier-Postposition for Equi-NP Deletion are illustrated by (15) and (16).

(15) a. Each of the men$_i$ tried [for each of the men$_i$ to drink a beer]$_{S_1}$
      b. Each of the men tried to drink a beer.
      c. The men each tried to drink a beer.

Sentences (15b) and (15c) can be derived from (15a) without difficulty. Equi-NP Deletion applies on the matrix cycle, eliminating the embedded subject, and Quantifier-Postposition applies optionally to the matrix subject. Since Quantifier-Postposition is optional, however, it could apply to the embedded subject on the S_1 cycle and optionally fail to apply to the matrix subject on the matrix cycle. The identity condition would no longer be satisfied and the result would be (16):

(16) *Each of the men tried for the men each to drink a beer.

In the case of predicates such as *want,* a similar result is obtained, where the coreferentially marked NP's cannot be so interpreted.

(17) *Each of the men$_i$ wants the men$_i$ each to drink a beer.

Since Quantifier-Postposition is optional, there is no natural way of ensuring that it will apply only if Equi-NP Deletion should later apply. Consequently there is no way of blocking (16) and (17) short of an ad hoc condition on Quantifier-Postposition.

If we assume that Dougherty's formulation of Quantifier-Postposition is wrong and that *the men each* forms a constituent, the ad hoc condition can be recorded as follows:

(18) If Quantifier-Postposition applies to a coreferential NP, it must apply to its controller.

Such a condition, though clearly ad hoc, would ensure that the matrix subject be identical to the embedded subject, and hence Equi-NP Deletion would apply in all cases.

There is some evidence that Quantifier-Postposition is more general than Dougherty's formulation. For example, consider the following sentences:

(19) a. We persuaded each of the men to drink a beer.
      b. We persuaded the men each to drink a beer.

(20) a. We gave each of the men a glass of beer.
      b. We gave the men each a glass of beer.

Since there is no movement of a subject from an embedded S to the matrix S containing predicates such as *persuade* in the standard theory, cf. [36: 22–23], rule (13) will not suffice to relate (19a) and (19b). Similarly (13) could not be utilized to relate (20a) and (20b). We should certainly strive to relate all the pairs in (10–12), (19), and (20) by a single rule; so we must conclude that Dougherty's formulation is too restrictive.

The argument advanced above for the cyclicity of Quantifier-Postposition depended on Dougherty's formulation of it. Since (13) cannot stand as formulated, we must ask if Quantifier-Postposition is indeed cyclic. If it is not, then perhaps the ungrammatical (16) and (17) could be circumvented by ordering Equi-NP Deletion before Quantifier-Postposition. There is, however, one observation which indicates that Quantifier-Postposition is cyclic. It is sometimes noted that cyclic transformations are those which are not root transformations in the sense of [54]. Since Quantifier-Postposition is quite obviously not a root transformation, I conclude that it is cyclic.[5] Moreover, the specific question of the cyclicity of Quantifier-Postposition is not that important for the more basic issue of concern here, since the argument can be generalized to any optional cyclic transformation. Taking Dative-Movement to be a representative optional cyclic transformation, as argued in [75], the point can be illustrated by the device of embedding relative clauses in the relevant NP's.

(21) a. [the boy [the boy gave a dime to Mary]$_{S_2}$]$_{NP_i}$ tried
          [for [the boy [the boy gave a dime to Mary]$_{S_1}$]$_{NP_i}$ to leave

      b. The boy who gave a dime to Mary tried to leave.
      c. The boy who gave Mary a dime tried to leave.

Both of the sentences (21b) and (21c) derive from (21a). In the case of (21b) Dative-Movement does not apply. In the derivation of (21c), however, Dative-Movement must apply on both the S_1 and S_2 cycles followed by Equi-NP Deletion on the matrix cycle.[6] Now Dative-Movement is an optional rule. Therefore the possibility arises of applying Dative-Movement on the S_1 cycle, but not on the S_2 cycle. In this event, the following ungrammatical string is generated:

(22) * The boy who gave a dime to Mary tried for the boy who gave Mary a dime to leave.

A similar result is obtained with predicates such as *want* where the identically indexed NP's cannot be interpreted as coreferential.

(23) * [the boy who gave a dime to Mary]$_{NP_i}$ wants [the boy who gave Mary a dime]$_{NP_i}$ to leave.

Thus, the ad hoc condition (18) will have to be generalized to all optional transformations, but this generalizing of the condition does not make it any less ad hoc.

(24) If an optional rule applies to a coreferential NP, it must apply to its controller.

Problems of a somewhat different nature for analyses incorporating Equi-NP Deletion arise in connection with predicates such as *try, condescend, attempt, need,* and the like. Within the standard theory, (25b) is derived from (25a).

(25) a. John$_i$ tried [for John$_i$ to leave]$_S$
      b. John tried to leave.

Now if *John$_i$* can be generated in complement subject position of (25), we expect *Mary, Henry, John$_j$* etc., also to be generated in this position. But such is not the case, as (26) amply illustrates.

(26) a.   *John tried for Mary to leave.
      b.   *John tried for Henry to leave.
      c.   *John$_i$ tried for John$_j$ to leave.

In order to account for this gap in what should be expected, a special constraint is required to ensure that the subject of the embedded sentence be identical to, and coreferential with, the subject of the matrix sentences in all such cases involving *try, condescend,* etc.

Similar problems emerge in conjunction with predicates such as *persuade* and *convince*. Within the framework of the standard theory, (27b) derives from (27a) by Equi-NP Deletion, cf. [39], [36: 22–23].

(27) a.   John persuaded Mary$_i$ [for Mary$_i$ to leave]
      b.   John persuaded Mary to leave.

Given a deep structure such as (27a), we expect that noncoreferential NP's should be generable in complement subject position. However, once again, the expected is not tolerated.

(28) a.   *John persuaded Mary for Harry to leave.
      b.   *Hubert convinced Sue for Martha to resign.

Again there is a necessity for a special condition that will ensure that the complement subject is identical to, and coreferential with, the object of predicates such as *persuade* and *convince*.

These observations are, of course, well known, although what they show is not widely recognized. Thus, Rosenbaum in [134: 95] cites several such examples and remarks that there "may well be an explanation for the necessary identity of erasing and erased noun phrases . . . , but this issue will not be taken up in the present study." Others, for example, both Lakoff and Perlmutter, in [90] and [113], attempt to solve the problem, but, in fact, do little more than redescribe it. Lakoff claims that *try, condescend,* etc. are exceptional with respect to Equi-NP Deletion. But Lakoff's conception of exceptionality, apparently influenced by ideas due to Postal, encompasses exceptional devices that were never permitted in

94

the standard theory. Thus, Lakoff marks predicates such as *try* and *persuade* with ad hoc absolute exception features so that they will obligatorily meet the structural description of Equi-NP Deletion. But clearly this is simply a reformulation of the problem and is tantamount to giving up the quest for an explanation for the ungrammaticality of (26) and (28).[7] Moreover it fails on independent grounds. For example, (29a) satisfies the absolute exception mechanism of Lakoff and will give rise to (29b).

(29) a. John$_i$ persuaded Mary [for John$_i$ to leave]
      b. John persuaded Mary to leave.

Not only does Lakoff fail to provide an explanation for the relevant observations, he fails to attain the level of observational adequacy.

    Perlmutter's proposal does not fare any better. He proposes two "deep structure constraints," a subject-subject constraint for predicates such as *try,* and an object-subject constraint for predicates such as *persuade.* Although Perlmutter never formalizes these constraints, they are intended to be well-formedness conditions on deep structures. Again it would seem that the bestowal of the appellation "deep structure constraint" upon the ad hoc conditions should not hide the fact that we have here another name for the problem. A redescription of the problem in terms of deep structure constraints does not amount to an explanation. In addition, whereas Perlmutter avoids the problem which Lakoff failed to confront vis-à-vis (28), his approach is nevertheless vitiated in view of examples like (30).

(30) a. John tried to be examined by the doctor.
      b. I persuaded John to be examined by the doctor.

In the standard deep structure of (30), the complement subject is not identical to the matrix subject or object. It is only after the complement has been passivized that the embedded subject satisfies the conditions for Equi-NP Deletion. Therefore, such examples constitute evidence against the *deep-structure* subject-subject and object-subject constraints. To overcome examples such as these, Perlmutter proposed more abstract deep structures along the lines of (31).

(31) a. John$_i$ tried [for John$_i$ $\left\{ \begin{array}{l} \text{let} \\ \text{get} \end{array} \right\}$ [the doctor examine John$_i$]s]s

b. I persuaded John$_i$ [for John$_i$ $\{ {}^{let}_{get} \}$ [the doctor examine John$_i$]$_S$]$_S$

However, as so often happens when more abstract syntactic structures are posited, the abstraction raises more problems than it solves. Thus, catastrophically, Perlmutter must require a rule which will delete the *let-get* clause in (31) in order to arrive ultimately at (30). Although Perlmutter fails to formulate this putative rule, Newmeyer [110: 202] points out that there will be an unresolvable difficulty with any formulation; namely, how is one to avoid applying the putative rule to (32a) to give (32b)?[8]

(32) a. I tried [for I $\{ {}^{let}_{get} \}$ [the doctor to examine you]$_S$]$_S$

      b. *I tried you to be examined by the doctor.
      c. I tried to get the doctor to examine you.

Since (32c) is grammatical and (32a) does not violate the deep structure constraint on *try,* there is no explanation within Perlmutter's framework for why the *let-get* clause cannot be deleted from (32a) to yield (32b), just as Perlmutter requires it to apply to (31a) to yield (30a). And there is, incidentally, a further difficulty. What is to ensure that the embedded clause is passivized so that (30a) is derived after the putative rule has deleted the *let-get* clause of (31a)? That is, what is to block (33)?

(33) *John$_i$ tried the doctor to examine John$_i$.

Fodor [62] concludes that Perlmutter must ultimately adopt a derived like-subject constraint, one which is reminiscent of Lakoff's absolute exception mechanism; she provides additional arguments against (31) as the source of (30).[9] Unfortunately, however, Fodor incorrectly concludes that there is indeed a need for a derived like-subject constraint and criticizes Newmeyer for attempting to eliminate any such constraint. Like Perlmutter, Fodor fails to formulate her like-subject constraint explicitly, but presumably she intends that the subject-subject and object-subject conditions of Perlmutter must be satisfied at some point in the course of the derivation, instead of in deep structure as in Perlmutter's approach. This proposal does not fare much better than Lakoff's or Perlmutter's in view of the following examples:

(34) a. John$_i$ tried [for the doctor to examine John$_i$]$_S$

    b.   John$_i$ tried [for John$_i$ to be examined by the doctor]$_S$

    c.   John tried to be examined by the doctor.

(35)   a.   John tried [for John$_i$ to examine the doctor]$_S$

    b.   *John$_i$ tried for the doctor to be examined by John$_i$

Although (34c) can be derived from (34a) since the derived like-subject constraint is satisfied in (34b), it will be possible to generate (35b) from (35a) since the derived like-subject constraint is satisfied in (35a). But (37a) is clearly ungrammatical and therefore such examples refute the derived like-subject constraint proposed by Fodor.

Fodor concludes her paper by asking the following question: "But why should there be an LSC [like-subject constraint] at all?" It will be clear in the sequel that I am claiming there is no like-subject constraint. Her rejection of Newmeyer's hypothesis is therefore unfounded.

To summarize, Lakoff's exception features, Perlmutter's deep structure constraints, and Fodor's like-subject constraint are all consequences of the unmotivated assumption that predicates such as *try* and *persuade* select S complements to which Equi-NP Deletion must apply. It should be clear that it is this assumption that is at the root of the problem. All three of the proposals, Lakoff's, Perlmutter's, and Fodor's, raise new problems, apparently necessitating further ad hoc accretions to linguistic theory, and should therefore be rejected.

A somewhat different ad hoc device is sometimes proposed to relate the following sentences:

(36)   a.   Sally expects herself to become rich some day.

    b.   Sally expects to become rich some day.

It is sometimes claimed that both (36a) and (36b) derive from a single underlying source. In this case the putative underlying source is (37).

(37)   Sally$_i$ expects [Sally$_i$ to become rich some day]$_S$

The procedure is then to permit Raising to apply optionally for predicates such as *expect,* although obligatorily for others. If Raising applies, (36a) is derived subsequent to Reflexivization. If Raising does not apply, Equi-NP Deletion is invoked to yield (36b). This new theoretical elaboration—that rules can be made optional for some lexical items and obligatory for others—is once again a consequence of the assumption that Equi-NP Deletion is a rule of English syntax. Part of the difficulty stems from the assumption that (36a) and (36b) should derive from the same source, but they should not, as I will argue below.

One additional principle which is at least in part a consequence of Equi-NP Deletion is the so-called convention of Pruning, which Ross in [138] describes as "a condition upon well-formedness of trees, which may operate at many points in a derivation of a sentence: whenever some configuration of rules produces a node S which does not branch, [Pruning] operates and deletes that node." Ross's initial formulation of Pruning is repeated as follows:

(38) Pruning: Delete any embedded node S which does not branch (i.e., which directly dominates only *NP* or *VP*).

If (38) is adopted, (39a) will become (39c) after first undergoing Equi-NP Deletion to give (39b).

(39) a. John$_i$ tried [John$_i$ [to leave]$_{VP}$]$_S$
      b. John tried [[to leave]$_{VP}$]$_S$
      c. John tried [to leave]$_{VP}$

In [138] Ross subsequently replaces (38) with a variant which inhibits the pruning of the embedded S in (39). But most linguists would agree that there is no embedded S in surface structure; the burden of proof is clearly on the proponent of the abstract structure to show that it is present in surface structure and Ross' evidence is weak.[10]

Above I noted in connection with predicates such as *try* and *persuade* that the standard theory of transformational grammar incorporating Equi-NP Deletion gives rise to gaps which some have tried to "account for" with absolute exception features, deep structure constraints, or derived like-subject constraints. The standard theory, which incorporates Equi-NP Deletion, also gives rise to gaps of another kind which evidently cannot be "accounted for." Consider the trivial fact that lexical predicates are subcategorized so as to select phrasal categories such as NP, AP, and S. For example, *pinch* selects NP, but not S. The lexical item *know* selects both S and NP, and so on. Facts about subcategorization are essentially idiosyncratic and are therefore relegated to the lexicon where idiosyncratic properties are most appropriately expressed; cf. [36]. Now, in addition to the phrasal categories NP, AP, PP, and S, there is the phrasal category VP. Certainly we would expect at least some predicates to be subcategorized so as to select VP. Yet the standard approach incorporating Equi-NP Deletion eliminates this otherwise expected phrasal category from the repertory of phrasal categories available for subcategorization, and, it should be added, VP is the only phrasal category so excluded. Clearly this gap is a consequence of the attempt to derive all instances of embedded VP's from S's by means of Equi-NP Deletion. I will record this fact as follows:

(40)   A lexical gap is created inasmuch as no VP complements are selected in deep structure.

Perhaps the strongest argument against Equi-NP Deletion is provided by examples given in [83] and [91]. King's observations are illustrated by the following examples excerpted from his article:

(41)   a.   Joan's taken more from you than Bill $\left\{ {has \atop *'s} \right\}$ _____ from me.

     b.   You'll need some and I $\left\{ {will \atop *'ll} \right\}$ _____ too.

     c.   I wonder where Gerald $\left\{ {is \atop *'s} \right\}$ _____ today.

     d.   We told him what a big boy you $\left\{ {are \atop *'re} \right\}$ _____ now.

Vowel-reduction and subsequent contraction are not possible if a noun phrase has been deleted or moved away from the otherwise reducible items; that is, contraction is prohibited before a removal site. A second set of contraction facts are adduced in [91]: the contraction of *want to, have to,* etc., to *wanna, hafta,* etc., is prohibited when *want* plus *to, have* plus *to,* etc., are made adjacent by removal of an NP.

(42)   a.   Teddy is the man I want _____ to beat Nixon.
     b.   *Teddy is the man I wanna beat Nixon.

In the standard theory, (42a) derives from approximately the following by movement or deletion of the NP following *want.*

(43)   Teddy is the man [I want the man to beat Nixon]$_S$

Since an element has to be moved away from *want,* leaving a removal site as in (42a), contraction cannot ensue, as in (42b). Now suppose we substitute in (43) *the man* for *Nixon* and *I* for *the man.* We obtain the following:

(44)   Teddy is the man [I want I to beat the man]

Now by Equi-NP Deletion the second instance of *I* will be deleted and the second instance of *the man* will be relativized, giving:

(45)   Teddy is the man I want _____ to beat _____.

But (45) is identical to (42a) with respect to the removal site following *want.* Therefore contraction should not be possible. Nevertheless, (46) disconfirms this prediction.

(46)   Teddy is the man I wanna beat.

If Equi-NP Deletion were really a transformation, we would expect it to behave as other transformations in blocking contraction. Since contraction is not blocked by Equi-NP Deletion, we must seriously question the existence of the latter. To save Equi-NP Deletion, a new ad hoc constraint would be required to block contraction from blocking in (45). By contrast, the possibility of contraction in (46) is a *consequence* of deriving it from a structure with a VP complement such as:

(47)   Teddy is the man [I want [to beat the man]$_{VP}$]$_S$

The significance of these examples was perceptively noticed by Baker:

> The failure of Equi-NP Deletion to leave behind a phonologically significant deletion site could be interpreted as suggesting the advisability of finding an alternative explanation for the facts which are accounted for by hypothesizing an underlying subject for infinitive phrases and a rule which deletes it. [7: 180]

A list of the ad hoc devices which are consequences of the rule of Equi-NP Deletion can now be given as (48).

(48)   i.   *there*-Insertion must not apply to coreferential NP's (= (9)).

ii.   If an optional rule applies to a coreferential NP, it must apply to its controller (=(24)).

iii.   Absolute exception features, deep structure constraints, or derived like-subject constraints are needed for predicates such as *try* and *persuade*.[11]

iv.   Optional versus obligatory application of Raising for predicates such as *expect*.

v.   S-Pruning (=(38)).

vi.   Lexical gap is created and no VP complements generated by base (=(40)).

vii.   A special constraint to block the blocking of contraction for the output of Equi-NP Deletion.

It will be recognized that all of these special conditions are a consequence of the assumption that the relevant predicates select S complements and that there is a rule of Equi-NP Deletion. The conditions are all ad hoc in the sense that they do not provide explanations for additional data, nor can they be generalized in any revealing way. An explanation would be a hypothesis eliminating the need for (48i–vii) altogether. The hypothesis I wish to advance has this effect. It is an extension of what I called the VP hypothesis in the preceding chapter. Where the standard theory adopts an S complement whose subject is eliminated by Equi-NP Deletion, I propose a VP complement, which is not dominated by an abstract S node. For example, under the VP hypothesis (49a) derives from (49b), and not from (49c) as in the standard theory.

(49)   a. John tried to leave.
        b. John tried [to leave]$_{VP}$
        c. John tried [for John [to leave]$_{VP}$]$_S$

A consequence of this proposal is that there is no rule of Equi-NP Deletion as traditionally conceived.[12]

Now let us consider the status of (48i–vii) within a framework incorporating the VP hypothesis. In the first place, (48i) is superfluous since, if there is no embedded subject, *there*-Insertion will not be applicable, and, consequently, strings such as (7) will not be derivable. By similar reasoning, it is clear that (48ii) is also unnecessary under the VP hypothesis. The question of blocking (16), (17), (22), and (23) therefore does not even arise since (15a) and (21a) are not possible deep structures. As for (48iii), it is also unnecessary under the VP hypothesis. If verbs such as *try* select VP complements and verbs such as *persuade* select NP VP complements, it follows that ungrammatical strings such as (26) and (28) will not be generated.

Turning to (48iv), we see that (36a) and (36b) do not derive from (37) under the VP hypothesis. If there is no rule of Equi-NP Deletion, (36a) and (36b) must have different underlying sources; each derives from an underlying structure essentially identical to its surface structure. Omitting irrelevant details, the sources are approximately the following:

(50)   a.   Sally expects herself [to become rich]$_{VP}$
       b.   Sally expects [to become rich]$_{VP}$

This is in fact a desirable result as is evidenced by the fact that (50a) and (50b) are not synonymous as is implied by (37) in conjunction with (48iv). Additional contexts can serve to clarify this difference:

(51)   Sally expects herself to be dancing in her dreams, although she herself does not expect to be dancing.

Note that in (51) Mary can reflect upon herself and function as the object of her expectation. It is a consequence of the VP hypothesis that (50a) and (50b) have differing underlying sources and therefore should not be synonymous, a prediction which is borne out.[13]

Moving now to (48v), it is obvious that, if there is no abstract S node in the first place, there is no need to invoke a principle to arrive at the VP we start out with. It is equally obvious that there is no lexical VP gap under the VP hypothesis and hence no need for (48vi).

In connection with (48vii), it is important to note that the VP hypothesis, as contrasted with the standard theory, makes a prediction which is confirmed by the facts. Since there is no subject deleted by Equi-NP Deletion, the VP hypothesis *predicts* that (45) is contractable, a prediction that is borne out by (44), and that (42a) is not contractable, a prediction which is again borne out by (42b). By contrast, the standard theory predicts that neither (45) nor (42a) is contractable, a false prediction. Therefore the special constraint embodied in (48vii) is unneeded under the VP hypothesis.

To sum up, all of the data accounted for by (48i–vii) within the standard theory can be accounted for by a single hypothesis within the framework advocated here. Consider, for example, the following two ungrammatical strings:

(52) a.   *A few boys tried for there to be a few boys in class on time.
      b.   *A few boys tried for John to be in class on time.

The ungrammaticality of (52a) is accounted for by (48i) and the ungrammaticality of (52b) is accounted for by (48iii). Two distinct principles are summoned to rule out what can be ruled out by a single assumption—the VP hypothesis.

That all of the data described by (48i–vii) can be explained by the VP hypothesis is not surprising when we consider the function of most of the principles catalogued above. These principles "conspire" to yield a surface VP in place of the postulated abstract S. Now, if transformations such as *there*-Insertion and Dative-Movement are allowed to apply to the putative S complements, Equi-NP Deletion will not always apply, and the VP will not be obtained—hence (48i) and (48ii). If the subject of the putative S complements is not identical to the subject of *try*, or the object of *persuade*, Equi-NP Deletion will be inapplicable, and the required VP will not stand in place of the abstract S—hence (48iii). If pruning fails to apply, the surface VP will not take the place of the abstract S—hence (48v), and so forth. The conditions listed under (48) are thus in large part designed to preserve the abstract S. If the assumption that this S exists is abandoned, the principles are no longer needed and the body of examples described by the multifarious conditions is thereby explained under one general hypothesis. I therefore conclude that there is no abstract S in the range of cases investigated, and that, consequently, Equi-NP Deletion is not a rule of English grammar.[14]

5.3 APPARENT ALTERNATIVES TO THE VP HYPOTHESIS

Before turning to the putative arguments for Equi-NP Deletion and to some of the consequences of the VP hypothesis, I would like to examine briefly some attempts to preserve the abstract S of the relevant range of complement structures.

In some recent work the embedded complements are analyzed as S's with dummy symbols such as PRO or Δ as subjects; cf. [44], [75]. Such analyses are clearly superior to that criticized above inasmuch as they avoid the problems which necessitate (48i–ii). However, the problems giving rise to (48iii) simply reappear in another form. That is, it is necessary to ensure that PRO or Δ occupy the subject position of complements to *try, attempt,* etc., as well as the subject position of complements to *persuade, convince,* etc. Consequently, advocates of the dummy hypothesis will not give a unitary explanation for the ungrammaticality of both of the following examples:

(53) a. * A few boys wanted for there to be (Δ) in class on time.
     b. *A few boys tried for John to drink a beer.

The ungrammaticality of (53a) will presumably be due to the nonapplicability of *there*-Insertion to dummy subjects, but the ungrammaticality of (53b) will be due to the condition ensuring that dummy be the embedded subject in complements to *try.* By contrast, the VP hypothesis subsumes the ungrammaticality of both (a) and (b), thereby explaining it.

There is a further difficulty with the dummy hypothesis. What is to block the following?

(54) a. John_i wanted $[\text{John}_i \text{ to leave}]_S$
     b. John_i wanted $[\text{he}_i \text{ to leave}]_S$

The question arises of how to avoid generating an embedded subject coreferential to the matrix subject.

Finally, since there is no dummy in the surface structure of any S, it is apparently necessary to adopt a special rule to delete dummy or a special convention to express this fact. Now we must ask why elimination of dummy does not inhibit contraction, just as elimination (by deletion or movement) of lexical items inhibits contraction; cf. (42b) vs. (46) in the preceding section. Perhaps the response would be that elimination of dummy follows contraction. Since dummy has not been deleted in (55), contraction is possible, i.e., there is no removal site.

(55) I want Δ to go.

However, it is not obvious that the presence of the dummy symbol will not itself block contraction, as it does in (41) in, for example, Jackendoff's framework, where dummy must be present as implied by his extended lexical hypothesis, which disallows deletions.

104

The foregoing remarks should not be interpreted as a commitment to the nonexistence of dummy. Rather, the point is that dummy does not solve the problems outlined in section 5.2 and therefore the facts do not constitute evidence for dummy or against the VP hypothesis. I take no position here on the existence of dummy, although it should be observed that dummy is not utilized in the reanalysis sketched in Chap. 6, Section 2. Advocates of Δ and/or PRO are at least obliged to motivate it (them) in the full range of NP positions, not just in the subject position, and to show that dummy behaves identically with respect to contraction in all environments, or else they must offer a convincing explanation (or even description) for the asymmetry. Let us also note that Jackendoff, who operates with dummy, adopts a pruning convention in [75] for predicates such as *expect*. This convention is, of course, a consequence of his attempt to preserve the abstract S. Thus (48v) is adopted. It is also worth noting that preservation of the S with dummy gives rise to the gap indicated in (48vi).

A second attempt to preserve the abstract S is to adopt a global formulation of identity, such as the following:

(56)   Two NP's are identical if they are structurally identical and coreferential in deep structure.

The possibility of a global formulation of identity was first mentioned by Lees in [98: 75–76] and a formulation similar to (56) is suggested by Chomsky in [39: 28–30].[15] Like the previously discussed attempt to preserve the abstract S, the global formulation avoids the difficulties raised in connection with (16) and (22) and thus eliminates the need for (48ii). But (56) cannot account for the facts which give rise to the other conditions in (48), so there seems to be little gained by the global formulation of identity.[16]

A third attempt to preserve the abstract S meets with partial success but raises as many problems as it solves. The idea is to generate internal S's with boundary symbols, i.e., #S#, and to adopt the filtering function of transformations as outlined in [36: 137–39]. Deletion transformations such as Equi-NP Deletion are then formulated in a manner analogous to Relative-Clause–Formation [36: 137–38], i.e., so as to delete the internal occurrences of # in addition to the embedded subject (in this particular case). All strings with internal occurrences of # after transformations have applied are filtered out—that is, rejected as well-formed strings. This alternative to the VP hypothesis succeeds in eliminating several of the conditions of (48). For example, under the filtering approach the following will correspond to (53a) and (53b):

(57) a. A few boys tried #for there to be a few boys in class on time#
       b. A few boys tried #for John to drink a beer#

Although *there*-Insertion has applied to the complement of (57a), the boundary symbols have not been deleted by Equi-NP Deletion. Hence (57a) is filtered. Equi-NP Deletion is not applicable to (57b) since identity is not satisfied. Therefore, the boundary symbols are not deleted, and (57b) is filtered. The need for conditions (i–iii) of (48) is thus obviated.[17] However, the filtering approach fails to solve the contraction phenomena and apparently entails the lexical gap represented by (48vi). It would appear that a convention for pruning is also necessary—(48v). Moreover, problems of another kind arise in connection with the filtering approach. If internal S's are generated with boundary symbols, the following strings will be generated:

(58) a. I know #that John will leave#
       b. #That John is smart# is not obvious

The standard theory does not employ deletion transformations comparable to Equi-NP Deletion or Relative-Clause–Formation in the derivation of

(59) a. I know that John will leave.
       b. That John is smart is not obvious.

However, (58a) and. (58b) underlie (59a) and (59b) in the filtering framework. Since no deletion transformations apply to (58), the internal # will not be deleted, and thus (58a) and (58b) are filtered, resulting in no derivations giving rise to (59). To generate (59), new ad hoc boundary deletion rules are required which apparently serve no other purpose than to account for strings which the VP analysis would predict as grammatical without elaboration of theory. (Notice that the ad hoc deletion rules must somehow avoid deleting the boundary symbols in (57).)

In this section I have considered three apparent alternatives to the VP hypothesis. It appears that none is a viable alternative. In view of this conclusion, it will be well to turn to the evidence adduced in support of

Equi-NP Deletion in the literature. These arguments are taken up in the following section.

5.4 APPARENT ARGUMENTS FOR EQUI-NP DELETION

In the opening paragraph of this chapter I cited a typical assertion to the effect that "there is a transformation, called Equi-NP Deletion . . ." [105]. However, one would like to have more than dogma; in this case, one welcomes the putative syntactic arguments offered in support of the syntactic rule of Equi-NP Deletion. Therefore, in this section we ask the question—why is the rule of Equi-NP Deletion taken to be part of the transformationalists' repertory of transformations in the first place?

One of the basic arguments appears to be semantic in character. Consider by way of example the following:

(60)   John was persuaded to leave.

Chomsky cites (60) and writes, "The deep structure underlying this sentence must indicate that the subject-predicate relation holds in an underlying proposition of the form of (61) . . ." [39: 36].

(61) $[[\text{John}]_{\text{NP}}[\text{leave}]_{\text{VP}}]_{\text{S}}$

The claim, then, is that a complement preserving the abstract S is part of the underlying representation of (60), to which Equi-NP Deletion must then apply to yield (60). Chomsky's adoption of the abstract S is clearly based on his definitions of grammatical relations. Thus, he remarks that (61) must be part of the deep structure of (60) "assuming grammatical functions to be represented in the same manner suggested earlier . . ." [39: 36]. The earlier suggestion is that we understand "the relation 'subject-of' to hold between a phrase of the category noun phrase (NP) and the sentence (S) that directly dominates it, and the relation 'predicate-of' to hold between a phrase of the category verb phrase (VP) and the sentence that directly dominates it . . ." [39: 29–30]. Thus, the subject-predicate relation holds between an NP and predicate just in case both are *directly dominated* by the same S. In example (60), under this definition *John* is the subject of *persuade* and is furthermore the subject of *leave* only if there is an abstract S which directly dominates both *John* and *leave*. Hence (61), and Equi-NP Deletion as a consequence.

All other things being equal, abstract structures such as (61) as embeddings for (60) are only as good as the definitions of grammatical relations used as support for them. If the definitions employing "direct domination" of S can be supplanted with alternative definitions (perhaps of a more surface character), then grammatical relations can no longer be used to justify the abstract S complements. That a new definition is indeed necessary follows at once from Bresnan's results concerning sentences such as (62a), as she shows in [19], where (62a) must derive from a structure similar to (62b).[18]

(62) a. It is easy for Mary to please John.

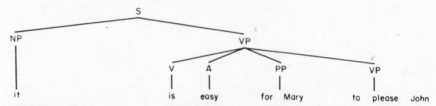

Although *Mary* is the subject of the embedded complement, the standard definition of subject fails to express this fact. There is, therefore, independent evidence indicating that a new definition of grammatical relations is needed which does not make use of the abstract S. This in turn implies that Equi-NP Deletion is not supported by grammatical relations.

The import of grammatical relations for Equi-NP Deletion is not explicitly discussed in the literature. On the other hand, in [125] Postal has attempted to provide what he considers to be independent evidence for the abstract S and concludes that it, together with the rule of Equi-NP Deletion, "is thus most strongly supported." Actually none of Postal's arguments are valid, and, in fact, his approach leads to a significant loss of generalization, as I will point out directly.

Postal's first argument is based on co-occurrence restrictions of the following sort.[19]

(63) a. *Joan dispersed.
       b. Joan got married.

(64) a. *Joan wants to disperse.
       b. Joan wants to get married.

Postal marks (63a) and (64a) as ungrammatical (although I would prefer to call the deviance semantic anomaly). The argument is that the semantic anomaly of (64a) would follow as a consequence of the semantic anomaly of (63a) if (64a) were derived from (65).

(65)   Joan wants [Joan disperse]$_S$

Similarly, the semantic well-formedness of (64b) would follow from the semantic well-formedness of (63b) if (64b) were derived from a similar structure with abstract embedded S. These consequences would indeed follow from the rule of lexical insertion and related feature analysis proposed by Chomsky in [36]. In a sense, however, this argument harks back to Chomsky's definition of grammatical relations. What can be said, evidently, is that singular NP's such as *Joan* cannot serve as the subjects of verbs such as *disperse* with semantic impunity. In other words, predicates such as *disperse* require plural or compound subjects such as *the girls, the group,* etc. If the notion subject-of is expressed only as a function of NP directly dominated by an S, then clearly the abstract S is needed to make (64a) a consequence of (63a). But the subject-of relation need not be so expressed, and, as noted above, cannot, in light of Bresnan's results. An alternative definition making *Joan* the subject of *want* and the subject of *disperse* in (64) and (65), together with a theory of selectional restrictions based on this definition would account for (63a) and (64a), as well as (63b) and (64b), in a straightforward way. Therefore, examples (63) and (64) pose a problem for the correct definition of the relation subject-of and do not support the abstract S. Consequently, they cannot be used in support of Equi-NP Deletion.

As a preface to the second argument for Equi-NP Deletion, in [125: 445] we are told that "the rules of sentence formation must generate complements to full sentential form." Here, the point is that the grammar must generate (66) independently of any dispute over Equi-NP Deletion (since it is Raising which comes into play).

(66)   a.   Joan wants [Barbara to get married]$_S$
       b.   Joan wants [Lucille to visit Betty]$_S$

However, the embedded S is itself controversial in spite of Postal's assumption to the contrary. Within the framework expounded here, for example, (66b) is derived from (67).

(67)

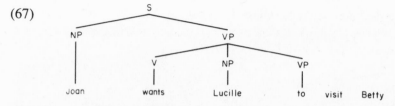

However, for the sake of argument, let us consider the virtue of Postal's argument under the assumption that (66) is analyzed with an embedded S. Postal's point is that, given (66), the requirement that an S be generated "is not an ad hoc addition to the grammar but, on the contrary, is necessarily part of the grammar on independent grounds" [125: 445]. The logic of this argument is less than clear. For, even if it is correct to generate S complements in (66), this would not imply that all complements to *want*-like predicates are S complements. To draw this conclusion is to make the same mistake that many generative semanticists have made in their program of reductionism. But Postal has in mind what he considers a more powerful argument for Equi-NP Deletion when he cites (66). He claims that there is "an interesting set of gaps in the class of sentences like" (66). Thus, he cites the following:[20]

(68) a. *Joan$_i$ wants *Joan$_i$ to get married.
      b. *The man$_i$ wants *the man$_i$ to get married.
      c. *We want *us to get married.
      d. *You want *you to get married.

Postal remarks, "the subject of the complement cannot be 'identical to' the subject of the main clause verb where 'identical' means coreferential" [125: 444]. He claims that (68a, b) "are illformed, or, at best, only interpretable in such a way that the italicized NP designate distinct beings" and that (68c, d) "are clearly illformed, just because the reference of the pronominal forms is relatively fixed" [125: 445]. Since sentences such as (66) exist in which noncoreferential NP's occur in the relevant positions, Postal considers the absence of (68) to constitute a gap which is filled by generating (68) and deriving (69) from (68).

(69) a. Joan wants to get married.
      b. The man wants to get married.
      c. We want to get married.
      d. You want to get married.

110

Thus, Postal argues that it is just the sentences of (68) that fill the gap at a more abstract level of representation, the superficial difference being due to the effects of Equi-NP Deletion. He writes,

> The idea that sentences with subjectless complements are derived by a deletion rule operating on NP somehow marked as being coreferential to main clause NP is thus most strongly supported. Such an analysis immediately explains the gaps in the set of complements with subjects. That is, it shows that these gaps, which involve coreference to an NP in a higher sentence, are exactly filled by the set of subjectless complements.   [125]

Postal's gap argument can be found in his earlier [122], where the more surface approach of Longacre is ridiculed. Like his first argument for Equi-NP Deletion and the associated S-structure, this argument is specious. In fact, here Postal's account can be shown to lead to a significant loss of generalization. For in Postal's framework, there is no way of generalizing the ill-formedness of (68) with that of (70).

(70)   a.   *$Joan_i$ wants $Joan_i$
           b.   *The man_i wants *the man_i*
           c.   *We* want *us*.
           d.   *You* want *you*.

Notice that the impossibility of (70) cannot be accounted for by recourse to Equi-NP Deletion, since there is clearly no sentential complement to *want* in these cases. Thus, Postal must rule out (70) by one criterion (e.g., Reflexivization) and (68) by a second distinct criterion (i.e., Equi-NP Deletion). But clearly whatever criterion is brought to bear to rule out (70) can be brought to bear in ruling out (68). But this refutes the argument for Equi-NP Deletion, since Equi-NP Deletion cannot express the obvious generalization. Sentences such as (68) cannot, therefore, be used to support Postal's contention that there is a rule of Equi-NP Deletion.

Postal's data can in fact be turned against him to support the VP hypothesis. For, if (68a–d) assume structures similar to (67), they will be identical to the structures assigned to (70) *modulo* the NP direct object complement. Therefore, rules requiring that pronouns be reflexive in simplex S's can be brought to bear in both cases to secure a violation.

It must be further noted that we find examples directly refuting Postal's gap argument, such as:

(71) a. I wanted to turn back.
      b. I wanted myself to turn back.

Some speakers apparently find (71b) strange, but this is evidently a reflection of their inability to create an appropriate context. It would be appropriate to use (71b) under circumstances in which the subject has no control over his actions as, for example, in *I imagined that I was on my way to the moon and as much as I wanted myself to turn back, I could not.*[21] Now, since (71b) derives from (72) in Postal's framework, his gap is a fortiori imagined.

(72) I wanted [I turn back]$_S$

Finally, let us not overlook a further observation which vitiates Postal's gap argument. Not only does Equi-NP Deletion imply the lexical gap represented as (48vi), but predicates such as *try* imply a gap of the type abhorrent to Postal. Thus, it is possible to again cite the nonoccurrence of examples such as:

(73) a. *Joan tried for Barbara to get married.
      b. *Joan tried for Lucille to visit Betty.

Here there are no corresponding grammatical sentences with S complements where the embedded subject is not identical to the matrix subject. In Postal's framework, however, *Joan tried to get married* derives from *Joan$_i$ tried [Joan$_i$ get married]* where the embedded and matrix subjects are identical and coreferential. But this creates a gap in subject position of the embedded complement in Postal's sense of gap, for if matrix and constituent subjects can be coreferential, we would also expect that they could be noncoreferential. If gaps can be used to argue for abstract structure, it would seem that gaps could be used to argue against it. Here then is further evidence against the abstract S and for the VP hypothesis, for there is no gap in this framework.

Postal's third argument for Equi-NP Deletion turns on Reflexivization. He cites the following examples:

(74) a. Bill's shaving himself annoyed me.
      b. *Shaving himself annoyed me.
      c. Shaving myself annoyed me.

Postal argues that the ungrammaticality of (74b) would follow from the ungrammalticality of (75) if it were derived from (75) by Equi-NP Deletion.

(75)   *My shaving himself (annoyed me)

Similarly the grammaticality of (74c) would follow from the grammaticality of *My shaving myself* (*annoyed me*) if the latter were its source and Equi-NP Deletion were a rule.

It is sufficient to note that reflexives should be generated in the base, as has been argued in various papers, and that reflexives, unlike most other pronouns, must have antecedents. The antecedent of *himself* in (74b) is *me*, which constitutes a violation of person concord, and the antecedent of *myself* in (74c) is *me*, which involves no such violation. Notice that (75) suffers from the same kind of violation as (74b) and that *My shaving myself*, like (74c), represents no such violation. Since the relevant pairs are treated in an analogous fashion, these data cannot be used as evidence for Equi-NP Deletion.

Finally, Postal [125] takes the appearance of reflexives in sentences such as (76) to be evidence for Equi-NP Deletion.

(76)   a.   Harry wants to justify himself.
       b.   Harry wants to visit his own father.

Postal remarks that "the possibility of reflexive forms and *own* possessives in such subjectless complements reveals the existence of underlying subjects" [125: 104]. Actually (76) constitutes no evidence for an underlying subject in deep structure. In fact, given the traditional intrasentence constraint on reflexives, which Postal adopts, one would expect *himself* and *his own* to appear in the complements if these complements were VP. What must be explained is not (76), but rather the following:

(77)   a.   John persuaded Mary to wash herself.
       b.   *John persuaded Mary to wash himself.

Under the standard theory, (77b) is not possible because *Mary* is the underlying subject of an abstract S complement *Mary to wash himself*. Within the theory being promoted here, there is no abstract S complement and we might adopt Emonds' suggestion that a reflexive NP_i must have an antecedent which is in some grammatical relation to the same verb or head as is NP$_i$. It will be seen in section 2 of chapter 6 that (77) is accounted for in a straightforward fashion without recourse to an abstract S complement. Emonds' suggestion explains not only (77), but also the following:

(78) a.   The father of Mary hated himself.
     b.   *The father of Mary hated herself.

(79) a.   Mary's father convinced himself.
     b.   *Mary's father convinced herself.

(80) a.   Sue threw the shoes behind her.
     b.   *Sue threw the shoes behind herself.

(81) a.   The girls saw at least fifteen balloons behind them.
     b.   *The girls saw at least fifteen balloons behind themselves.

In (78) *father* is the head of the antecedent NP and bears the grammatical relation subject-of to the predicate *hate*. Hence *himself* is here appropriate, whereas *herself* is not tolerated. In (80) *behind her* falls outside the scope of the verb *throw*, and likewise for *behind herself*, so that the latter constitutes a violation of the aforementioned constraint on reflexives.

In conclusion, Postal has provided no evidence in support of an abstract S-complement structure. Therefore, none of his data can be used in support of Equi-NP Deletion.

The only other explicit argument for Equi-NP Deletion that I am aware of in the literature is due to Peters [118]. Peters assumes that Equi-NP Deletion deletes NP's under structural identity as described above. His argument focuses on the following example:

(82)   Revealing corruption will proceed hand in hand with shaking up the government.

Peters remarks, "Let X represent the subject of *reveal* and Y the subject of *shake up*" [118: 376]. He then attempts to construct an argument for Equi-NP Deletion by letting $X = Y$'s *shaking up the government* and $Y = X$'s *revealing corruption*. Peters claims that (82) can be interpreted either as $Y = X$'s *revealing corruption* or as $X = Y$'s *shaking up the government*, but not simultaneously as both, which is taken as evidence for Equi-NP Deletion. However, I do not think there is any truth in the claim that X can

114

be interpreted as *Y's shaking up the government* or that *Y* can be interpreted as *X's revealing corruption*. Indeed, phrases such as *revealing corruption's shaking up the government* and *shaking up the government's revealing corruption* are ungrammatical, indicating that the putative sources should be rejected. Moreover, even if such structures were possible, the simultaneous equation could be easily prohibited by the alternative laid out in section 3 of chapter 6.

I think it is therefore fair to conclude that no evidence has been offered to support an abstract S complement and with it Equi-NP Deletion. When the arguments of the literature are subjected to critical review it appears that they do not support the standard theory. Indeed, in some cases they provide additional support for the VP hypothesis.

5.5   SOME CONSEQUENCES OF THE VP HYPOTHESIS

In section 5.2, I concluded that there is no rule of Equi-NP Deletion with associated abstract S and in section 5.4, I rejected the arguments which have been advanced in support of it. In this section I would like to turn to some of the consequences of this conclusion, which I repeat as Proposition I.

PROPOSITION I: There is no rule of Equi-NP Deletion.

In light of the evidence advanced in section 5.2, I take this proposition to be established. Let us now assume, without considering the evidence in support of it, that there is a rule of Object-Shift (= Tough-Movement), either in Postal's sense [126] or Berman and Szamosi's [12] or Bresnan's [19]. Recall that Object-Shift is posited to relate the following sentences:

(83)   a.   It is easy to please John.
       b.   John is easy to please.

Assuming that Object-Shift exists, consider the following:

(84)   a.   John tried to be easy to please.
       b.   John wants to be easy to please.

The derivation for (84a) would be something like the following in the standard theory. (If dummy is substituted for *it* in the complement to *try*, the argument is not affected.)

(85) John$_i$ tried [it to be easy to please John$_i$]$_S$ $\implies$ Object-Shift
      John$_i$ tried [John$_i$ to be easy to please] $_{[S}$ $\implies$ Equi-NP Deletion
      John tried to be easy to please.

If Object-Shift is a rule, to derive (83a), *John* must be the deep object of *please* and Object-Shift must promote it to the subject position of *be easy*. But this means that Equi-NP Deletion will be required to delete the second occurrence of *John$_i$*. However this implies that Equi-NP Deletion is a rule, contradicting Proposition I. Since Proposition I is true, I conclude that there is no rule of Object-Shift.[22]

   PROPOSITION II: There is no rule of Object-Shift.

   Let us now make a further assumption, again without considering the evidence in the literature for it. Let us assume that there is a rule of Passive which relates sentences such as the following:

(86) a. The doctor examined Mary.
      b. Mary was examined by the doctor.

Assuming that Passive is a rule, let us turn to the following:

(87) a. Mary tried to be examined by the doctor.
      b. Mary wants to be examined by the doctor.

Since *to be examined by the doctor* in (87) is a passive phrase, the standard theory derives (87) from more abstract structures with underlying S complements, as illustrated in (88).

(88) Mary$_i$ tried [for the doctor to examine Mary$_i$]$_S$ $\implies$ Passive
      Mary$_i$ tried [for Mary$_i$ to be examined by the doctor]$_S$ $\implies$
                                                    Equi-NP Deletion
      Mary tried to be examined by the doctor.

Again, if there is a rule of Passive, there is a rule of Equi-NP Deletion. But there is no rule of Equi-NP Deletion. Consequently there is no rule of Passive.

116

PROPOSITION III: There is no rule of Passive.

Let us now assume that there is a rule of Raising to Object Position (ROP). Such a rule has been proposed to yield derivations such as the following:

(89)   John expected [Mary to leave]$_S$ $\Longrightarrow$ ROP
       John expected Mary [to leave]$_S$

Assuming that such a rule exists, in deriving (90), we must employ a derivation similar to (91).

(90)   Mary was expected by Sam to leave.

(91)   Sam expected [Mary to leave]$_S$ $\Longrightarrow$ ROP
       Sam expected Mary [to leave]$_S$ $\Longrightarrow$ Passive
       Mary was expected by Sam to leave.

Thus, if there is a rule of Raising to Object Position, there is a rule of Passive, contradicting Proposition III, for if there were a rule of Passive, this would contradict Proposition I. Hence there is no rule of Raising to Object Position.

PROPOSITION IV: There is no rule of Raising to Object Position.

Continuing in this way let us assume that there is a rule of Raising to Subject Position (RSP). This rule has been proposed to relate (92a) and (92b).

(92)   a.   It appears that Mary is rich.
       b.   Mary appears to be rich.

Assuming that RSP exists, we wish to derive

(93)   a.   John tried to appear to be calm.
       b.   John wants to appear to be calm.

Such examples would have derivations such as the following:

(94) John$_i$ tried[it appear [John$_i$ to be calm]$_S$]$_S$ $\Longrightarrow$ RSP
     John$_i$ tried [John$_i$ appear [to be calm]$_S$]$_S$ $\Longrightarrow$

                                        Equi-NP Deletion

     John tried to appear to be calm.

The existence of Raising to Subject Position implies the existence of Equi-NP Deletion. Since Equi-NP Deletion does not exist, I conclude that Raising to Subject Position does not exist.

    PROPOSITION V: There is no rule of Raising to Subject Position.

    Now assume that there is a rule of Dative-Movement which relates the next two sentences:

(95)   a.   John gave a dime to Mary.
        b.   John gave Mary a dime.

If such a rule exists, (96) will have a derivation similar to (97).

(96)   Mary was given a dime.

(97)   PRO gave a dime to Mary $\Longrightarrow$ Dative-Movement
     PRO gave Mary a dime $\Longrightarrow$ Passive (and PRO-Deletion)
     Mary was given a dime.

We see that the assumption implies that Passive exists, contradicting Proposition III. Therefore Dative-Movement does not exist.

    PROPOSITION VI: There is no rule of Dative-Movement.

    Finally, the standard theory incorporates a rule of *there*-Insertion which relates the next pair:

(98)   a.   A cow is in the yard.
        b.   There is a cow in the yard.

Let us assume that *there*-Insertion exists. If so, (99) would be derived according to (100).

(99)   There was believed to be jelly between their toes.

(100)   PRO believed [jelly to be between their toes]$_s$ $\Longrightarrow$

there-Insertion

PRO believed [there to be jelly between their toes]$_s$ $\Longrightarrow$

ROP

PRO believed there [to be jelly between their toes]$_s$ $\Longrightarrow$

Passive

There was believed to be jelly between their toes.

Again, if *there*-Insertion exists, Passive exists, a contradiction. Therefore, *there*-Insertion is not a rule.

PROPOSITION VII: There is no rule of *there*-Insertion.

We see, then, that a good deal of syntax is balanced somewhat precariously on the putative rule of Equi-NP Deletion, which in turn is based, at least in part, on semantic criteria such as grammatical relations and selectional restrictions. If the supporting assumption is abandoned, it will certainly have a wholesale effect on the syntax at large. Therefore, these results might be interpreted as a reductio ad absurdum argument in favor of Equi-NP Deletion after all. Indeed, it seems peculiar that authors have not pointed to transformations such as Passive, Dative-Movement, and so forth as motivation for Equi-NP Deletion in the first place, since it is such syntactic facts which provide the strongest support for it. Before accepting the reductio interpretation, however, we must ask if there is not an alternative to the classical transformational account which has the advantage of avoiding the undesirable consequences of Equi-NP Deletion listed in (48). I think there are plausible alternatives, and I will explore two such alternatives in the following chapter.

NOTES TO CHAPTER 5

[1] According to Chomsky [36: 145], only "certain lexical items are designated as 'referential' " and indexed by "a general convention." Thus, two items may be strictly identical without bearing indices if they are not members of the special class of referential items.

[2] Unfortunately the "general convention" or indexing algorithm mentioned in n. 1 has never been made explicit, in spite of the fact that there is a good deal that rides on its exact formulation. According to [36: 145] "certain lexical items" are designated as referential, but we are not told which. Since NP's, and not N's, are

deleted by Equi-NP Deletion, it would seem that NP's should be designated as coreferential. However NP's are not lexical items, whereas N's are. If N's are marked as coreferential, we must explain the impossibility of generating (i).

(i)   The boy$_i$ with red hair wants the boy$_i$ with a black shirt to drink a beer.

According to [36: 146], "the semantic component will then interpret two referential items as having the same reference just in case they are strictly identical—in particular just in case they have been assigned the same integer in the deep structure." Since the relevant N's are strictly identical in (i) and since they are "lexical items," they will thus incorrectly be interpreted as coreferential. Clearly, then, the relevant categories for coreferentiality are not lexical items but, rather, larger categories such as NP. Therefore, it would appear that the indexing procedure must assign indices to NP's, but, here, structural identity would evidently be a condition for marking two NP's with identical indices. It would appear that there is a certain degree of redundancy built into this framework, for, structural identity is used twice—once in the explicit formulation of the indexing procedure, and once in the formulation of the principle of unique recoverability of deletion (or alternatively in the formulation of Equi-NP Deletion itself). If coreferentiality is viewed in a more interpretive framework and made irrelevant to the operation of transformations, as in the sequel, these problems are circumvented.

A second question arises in connection with the indexing procedure. There are apparently examples of deletion exemplified by the following.

(ii)   Sam saw Mary's dog on the street and Harry's _____ in the fountain.

Here an occurrence of *dog* has presumably been deleted under identity, but the two instances are not coreferential. Such cases have been called "identity of sense" deletion in [65]. What are the consequences of such examples for the indexing procedure and for unique recoverability of deletion? If the two instances of *dog* are not indexed, what formal device is to keep them from being indexed? Indexing cannot be optional inasmuch as (iii) could then be converted to (iv) by Equi-NP Deletion, since unique recoverability would not be violated due to the less restrictive nondistinctness convention adopted in [36: 177–182; 234, n. 38].

(iii)   Sam$_i$ wants Sam to drink a beer.
(iv)   Sam$_i$ wants to drink a beer.

The discussion seems to point to a more interpretive approach to deletion phenomena.

[3]Unique recoverability and the foregoing erasure principle are not equivalent since the former is designed to encompass deletion of "the designated representa-

tive of a category'' [35: 41], in addition to deletion under identity. Designated categories would allow for deletion of *you* by the imperative transformation, deletion of an unspecified agent of the passive, etc.

[4]The powerful device of SD-features advocated in [90] also fails in view of the fact that *want* complements are not affected by Equi-NP Deletion in cases such as *John wants Mary to leave.*

[5]It would seem that the distinction between cyclic transformations and post-cyclic (or last-cyclic) is a tenuous one, since root transformations by virtue of applying only to root S's can never display a cyclic effect. We might therefore conjecture that all transformations are cyclic, the noncyclic effect being due not to a theoretical term "post cyclic," but rather to the theoretical term "root transformation." In this connection it is interesting to contrast the practice of generative semanticists, who require an *ABA* type argument before admitting a rule to the cycle and others, who assume that all rules are cyclic unless proved post-cyclic. In section 5.5, I will suggest a somewhat different dichotomy.

[6]Note that strict cyclicity rules out the possibility of Equi-NP Deletion followed by Dative-Movement on S_2.

[7]In other words Lakoff claims that a whole class of semantically related predicates—*persuade, convince, urge,* etc.—is syntactically irregular for appearing in the structures in which they appear. In other words regularity is reduced to irregularity within Lakoff's framework. Cf. the discussion in chapter 2 of this text.

[8]See Newmeyer [110] for additional criticism of Perlmutter's constraints. See also Fodor [62] for additional arguments, where some of Newmeyer's criticism is repeated. Although I accept Newmeyer's rejection of the like-subject constraint, I do not agree with his conclusions concerning the alleged intransitivity of *begin.*

[9]Perlmutter's deep structure constraints do not appear in [114], which may indicate that he no longer holds the views of [113].

[10]Ross's revised principle is based on the assumption that the complementizer *to* is directly dominated by S_1, not by VP, an assumption for which evidence has never been offered. He also argues from Extraposition, but I do not accept his analysis of Extraposition, nor his position that it is not cyclic; cf. section 5.5.

[11]Condition (iii) actually amounts to two separate constraints. Also note that (i) and (ii) are global in the sense of Lakoff [91] and are therefore to be avoided, cf. Chap. 3.

[12]Some readers may wish to entertain the possibility of eliminating the abstract S complements for some predicates, e.g., *try, persuade,* etc., while preserving the abstract S for others, e.g., *want, expect,* etc., but I see no virtue in such a position since it does not explain all of (48).

[13]Postal seems to be unaware that self-reflection is possible in many cases. Thus, in [126] he claims that sentences such as *I seem to myself to be clever* are

ungrammatical. But this is clearly not the case (thereby refuting the Cross-Over Condition). See chap 1 for further relevant examples with *remind*.

[14]Let us punctuate this section by noting that *there*-Insertion as an argument against Equi-NP Deletion in the text is adapted from Bresnan [18], where analogous facts are adduced in refutation of a transformational analysis of pronominalization. The text method of using relative clauses and optional transformations can now be used to support her argument. Thus, if (i) derives from (ii) by a transformation of Pronominalization, what is to keep Dative-Movement from optionally applying on the S_1 cycle, but not on the S_2 cycle?

(i)   [The boy who gave a dime to Sally]$_{NP_i}$ $\begin{Bmatrix} \text{knew that she loved him}_i \\ \text{tried to kill himself}_i \end{Bmatrix}$

(ii)   [The boy [who gave a dime to Sally]$_{S_2}$]$_{NP_i}$ $\begin{Bmatrix} \text{knew that Mary loved} \\ \text{tried to kill} \end{Bmatrix}$

        [the boy [who gave a dime to Sally]$_{S_1}$]$_{NP_i}$

For additional arguments against the transformational analysis of pronouns, see [20], [50], [70], and [75]. Postal [129] purports to reply to [20], but all of his criticism was taken into account in the published version of [20]; cf. the editorial apology in [129]. Postal's [129] also gives a number of irrelevant arguments against Dougherty.

[15]The global innovation suggested by Lees and Chomsky is reserved for a single formal device—identity and, unlike the global rules of generative semantics, was proposed as a universal. These authors do not allow global devices as ad hoc rules as in recent papers by generative semanticists. Global proposals by generative semanticists are not convincing in view of their failure to treat a wide range of relevant facts in each case. The full set of relevant facts tends to vindicate the standard theory over the global approach, at least in all instances reported to date; cf. chapter 3.

[16]This remark should not be interpreted as an argument against global identity but rather that global identity is not supported by the phenomena under discussion. The fate of global identity must rest on the data brought in support of it in [98] and [39]. It is understandable that global identity should be proposed at a time when the relevance of interpretive rules for classical deletion phenomena had not been recognized (even though interpretive devices were already implicit in [32]). I think a good case against global identity can now be made in view of interpretive developments.

[17]The need for (48i) is actually not obviated since the *want/expect* cases allow Raising and therefore delete boundaries. Thus, *some boys*$_i$ *want there to be some boys*$_i$ *in class on time* should be fine. I am grateful to R. Huybregts for this observation.

[18]Compare the discussion of the preceding chapter.

[19]Actually such facts were mentioned as early as 1955 by Chomsky [32: chap. VII] with respect to both selectional restrictions and number agreement. For example, Chomsky notes the similarities between (i) and (ii) with respect to number agreement.

(i)   a.   John is an officer.
        b.   *John is officers.
        c.   *They are an officer.
        d.   They are officers.

(ii)   a.   John wants to be an officer.
        b.   *John wants to be officers.
        c.   *They want to be an officer.
        d.   They want to be officers.

[20]The gap argument for Equi-NP Deletion is explicitly given by Chomsky as early as 1955, cf. [32: chap. IX, 642 *passim*], although Postal fails to give credit. Both arguments are also given by Rosenbaum in [134].

[21]It would seem to be an error to consider such examples as somehow special, perhaps as being noncoreferential with respect to subject and reflexive pronoun. It seems obvious that it is the form of the sentence which determines the interpretation in this case.

[22]This argument is empirical in character; we cannot conclude on grounds of logic alone that there is no rule of Object-Shift since it is always possible to eliminate it for examples such as (84) and adopt it for simple sentences. The point is that this still leaves us with the problem of accounting for the fact that *John* is the object of *please* in (84) and that the device summoned to account for this fact should be available to account for the relatedness of (83a) and (83b), thus making Object-Shift in its classical formulation redundant. There will be some who will attempt to "generalize" Object-Shift or Object-Deletion to apply to sentences with predicates with *try* (with embedded VP complement), but this is clearly futile; cf. Passive below. (Others may resort to the false claim that sentences such as (87a) below are ungrammatical.) These remarks apply to all "proofs" of this section *mutatis mutandis*.

Chapter 6

Alternatives to the Standard Theory:
The Stratified Cycle vs. The Inverse Cycle

Given the framework of the (extended) standard theory, the conclusions concerning the nonexistence of the transformations discussed in the previous chapter would seem to follow. We are now faced with the choice of attempting to preserve the aforementioned transformations, and whatever advantages they encompass, by revising certain features of the underlying theoretical framework, or of accepting the conclusions and attempting to express the generalizations captured by the standard transformations in a new way. The first alternative is discussed in section 6.1 and the second alternative is explored in 6.2.†

6.1   THE STRATIFIED CYCLE HYPOTHESIS

By way of introduction to the stratified cycle, I will recapitulate an analysis of relative clauses I promoted some years ago in [14]; cf. [30], [44: fn. 70], [147].[1] Now, the standard theory derives relatives from sources with fully specified head nouns or noun phrases. For example, (1a) and (1b) are taken to be the structures underlying (2a) and (2b), respectively.

(1)   a.   [the book [Kurt put the book on the table]$_S$]$_{NP}$
      b.   [the speaker [Mary introduced the speaker]$_S$]$_{NP}$

(2)   a.   the book which Kurt put on the table
      b.   the speaker who(m) Mary introduced

The relative clause transformation is formulated so as to front the identical NP, which is simultaneously or subsequently converted into a relative pronoun, *which* in the case of inanimate NP's such as in (1a) and (2a), and *who(m)* in the case of animate NP's as in (1b) and (2b). Variations on this basic analysis may involve incorporating a Comp node in (1) with or without a pronoun substituted for the embedded NP in deep structure, so that Relative-Clause–Formation may take on the characteristics of a deletion transformation rather than a movement transformation. In contrast to these more traditional analyses, I suggested that relative clauses not bear fully specified heads in deep structure. The heads were rather a consequence of a "Raising" rule. Thus, the relatives (2b) were derived from the more basic (3) under the Raising analysis.

(3)   a. $[\Delta$ [Kurt put the book on the table]$_S$ NP]$_{NP}$
       b. $[\Delta$ [Mary introduced the speaker]$_S$]$_{NP}$

The evidence I provided in support of this analysis was similar to that which had been used in support of the Passive transformation.[2] Since the subcategorizational restrictions are expected to be invariant for corresponding actives and passives, an interesting test had been devised by Chomsky, Klima, and perhaps others to confirm the Passive transformation. The test was to consider the distribution of nouns which idiosyncratically follow certain verbs, such as *tabs*, as in *keep tabs on, heed,* as in *pay heed to,* etc. Such nouns exhibit a very limited distribution and are usually considered as idioms. Consider, for example, the following:

(4)   a. *The police maintained tabs on the students.
       b. *Joan directed little heed to the warning.

(5)   a. The police kept tabs on the students.
       b. John paid little heed to the warning.

Since nouns such as *tabs* and *heed* are associated with unique predicates, the following sentences were taken as evidence that passives must derive from actives:

(6)   a. Tabs were kept on the students.
       b. Little heed was paid to the warning.

In [14], I pointed out that a similar argument can be made for the Raising analysis of relative clauses. It is sufficient to consider a noun such as *headway,* which, like *tabs* and *heed,* is associated with a single predicate, in this case *make.*[3]

(7)   a. John made headway on his thesis.
       b. John made progress on his thesis.

(8) a. *John dislikes headway.
     b. John dislikes progress.

By parity of reasoning with the case of passives, I argued that examples such as the following support the promotion analysis of relative clauses:

(9) a. The headway that John made was substantial.
     b. *The headway that John disliked was substantial.

On the basis of the promotion analysis of relative clauses, I concluded that co-occurrence restrictions must be checked cyclically, whereas in the standard theory co-occurrence restrictions are not "checked" but rather accounted for by conditions on lexical insertion (cf. [14]) and of course lexical insertion is not cyclical in the standard theory. In the Raising theory, co-occurrence restrictions are checked in the relative clause before raising of the NP to the head position and, subsequently, on the cycle containing the head, so as to ensure that the matrix verb and the raised NP are compatible. Thus, the subcategorization checking on the embedded cycle ensures that (10a) is ill-formed, while the checking procedure on the matrix cycle ensures that (10b) is ill-formed.

(10) a. * Everyone enjoyed the cake that Mary slept.
      b. * Everyone slept the cake that Mary enjoyed.

Let us now return to the difficulties noted in earlier chapters in connection with Equi-NP Deletion. On the one hand, we would like to eliminate Equi-NP Deletion so as to provide for the simple [+_____VP], [+_____PP VP], [+_____NP VP], and other subcategorizations for examples such as *try, persuade, expect, be easy,* etc. On the other hand, we would like to retain Equi-NP Deletion so as to preserve such basic transformations as Passive, Dative-Movement, *there*-Insertion, and Raising to Subject Position. Faced with this dilemma, there seems to be no way to preserve the (extended) standard theory as it now stands. Suppose we therefore adopt a cyclic account of subcategorization, as in the Raising analysis of relative clauses (without, however, committing ourselves to such an analysis of relative clauses). Furthermore, let us partition the movement transformations into two classes, those applying to simple sentences, which I will call *simplex* rules (S-rules), and those applying across sentence boundaries, which I will call *embedding* rules (E-rules).[4]

Armed with these distinctions, we are able to suggest an alternative to the standard theory which circumvents much of the criticism leveled in chapter 5.

STRATIFIED CYCLE HYPOTHESIS: E-rules, Pruning, Co-occurrence checking, and S-rules apply in that order on each cycle.

The effect of this hypothesis for the relevant range of examples can now be illustrated. Consider first the following deep structures mentioned in chapter 5:

(11) a. [John tried [the doctor to examine John]$_{S_1}$]$_{S_0}$
      b. [John tried [Mary to leave]$_{S_1}$]$_{S_0}$

Taking (11a) first, we see that no E-rules are applicable on the S_1 cycle. The S-rule, Passive, can apply, but not before co-occurrence restrictions are checked, which, in this case, are satisfied. After Passive applies, we get:

(12) [John tried [John to be en examined by the doctor]]$_{S_0}$

On the S_0 cycle, one E-rule is applicable—Equi-NP Deletion. It applies, followed by Pruning, yielding:

(13) [John tried [to be examined by the doctor]$_{VP}$]$_{S_0}$

At this point co-occurrence restrictions are checked and it is seen that the subcategorization conditions associated with *try* are satisfied, since *try*, unlike some other predicates, selects a VP, not an S. We therefore succeed under the new hypothesis in deriving *John tried to be examined by the doctor*. A summary of this derivation is laid out in (14).

(14) [John tried [the doctor [to examine John]$_{VP}$]$_{S_1}$]$_{S_0}$
      1ST CYCLE:

      —————————— E-rules, Pruning
      no violation   Co-occurrence Check
      John to be en examine by the doctor   Passive

2ND CYCLE:

[John tried [[to be en examine by the doctor]$_{VP}$]$_{S_1}$]$_{S_0}$

                                                  Equi-NP Deletion

[John tried [to be en examine by the doctor]$_{VP}$]$_{S_0}$ Pruning

no violation   Co-occurrence Check

———————   *S*-rules

Consider now what would happen if the Passive transformation should fail to apply on the S_1 cycle. Equi-NP Deletion would then be inapplicable on the S_0 cycle, and we would thereby fail to satisfy co-occurrence restrictions since Pruning will also fail to yield the requisite VP. Similar remarks apply to (11b), which also leads to ill-formedness.

It is easy to see that, given the stratified cycle, sentences such as *John persuaded Mary to leave* can derive from structures similar to [*John persuaded Mary* [*Mary to leave*]$_{S_1}$]$_{S_0}$ and that *John persuaded Mary* [*Bill to leave*] will be blocked by means of co-occurrence checking, as in the case of (11b). It is also easy to see that examples such as the following will be blocked in a completely analogous fashion:

(15)   *A few students tried for there to be a few students in class on time.

In this way, objections (i–iv) of (48) in chapter 5 are met by the Stratified Cycle. The complete list of objections collected in chapter 5 is repeated for convenience of reference here as (16):

(16) i.   *there*-Insertion must not apply to coreferential NP's.

      ii.   If an optional rule applies to a coreferential NP, it must apply to its controller.

     iii.   Absolute exception features, deep structure constraints, or derived like-subject constraints are needed for predicates such as *try* and *persuade*.

     iv.   Optional versus obligatory application of Raising for predicates such as *expect*.

     v.   S-Pruning.

     vi.   Lexical gap is created and no VP complements generated in base.

     vii.   A special constraint to block the blocking of contraction for the output of Equi-NP Deletion.

Although it is true that objection (vi) still holds, it is to be noted that the gap is no longer lexical, since *try* etc., will be marked [+_____VP]; the gap is in phrase structure. Thus, the first conjunct of (vi) no longer applies to the stratified cycle. As for (vii), this objection can conceivably be overcome by recourse to strict cyclicity as suggested by Bresnan in [21]. The difference between *Teddy is the man I wanna beat Nixon* and *Teddy is the man I wanna beat* is held to be a violation of strict cyclicity in the case of application of Contraction to the former, but not the latter. To see this more clearly, consider the following derivation:

(17)   [Teddy is the man [I want [the man to beat Nixon]$_{S_2}$]$_{S_1}$]$_{S_0}$
       S_1-CYCLE:
       _____   Equi-NP Deletion
       _____   Contraction

       S_0-CYCLE:
       Teddy is the man [I want ϕ to beat Nixon]$_{S_1}$
                                     Rel. Clause Deletion
                    *wanna   Contraction

On the S_1 cycle, both Equi-NP Deletion and Contraction are inapplicable. On the S_0 cycle, however, Relative-Clause Deletion is applicable. It would appear that Contraction could then follow, but this would constitute a violation of strict cyclicity since Contraction is confined to material in S_1. By contrast, there is no violation of Strict Cyclicity in (18).

(18)   [Teddy is the man [I want [I to beat the man]$_{S_2}$]$_{S_1}$]$_{S_0}$
       S_1-CYCLE:
       I want ϕ to beat the man   Equi-NP Deletion
       I wanna beat the man   Contraction

       S_0-CYCLE:
       Teddy is the man I wanna beat ϕ Rel.-Clause Deletion

In (18) Strict Cyclicity is not violated, for, on the S_1 cycle, contraction is applicable and part of the contractable material is in the complement of S_2. Bresnan's analysis may therefore eliminate objection (vii) of (16) provided we assume that Contraction is cyclic and that the deletion site facts do not apply to contraction phenomena involving *to*.

We are thus left with (v) and a weaker form of (vi) as the remaining objections to the Stratified Cyclic Hypothesis. But I think it is clear that the stratified cycle is to be favored over the standard treatment of these data.

6.2   THE INVERSE CYCLE

In this section I will explore a more radical alternative to the standard theory than the stratified cycle. This alternative springs from an acceptance of the conclusions drawn in section 4 of chapter 5: that the VP hypothesis is sound and that consequently there are no rules such as Equi-NP Deletion, Object-Shift, Passive, Raising to Object Position, Raising to Subject Position, Dative-Movement, and *there*-Insertion. Although these transformations will be rejected in this section as classically formulated, this does not mean that there is nothing to account for. The attractiveness of the standard theory is due in part to the account it provides of facts such as the following: *Mary* is the object of *please* in (19a), as it is in (b); *apple* is the object of *eat* in both (c) and (d); *Sam* is the subject of *eat* in both (c) and (d); *cow* bears the same relation to *be in the yard* in (e) as it does in (f); *Bill* is the subject of *be smart* in (g); *fish* is the direct object of *give* in (h).

(19) a.   Mary is easy to please.
      b.   It is easy to please Mary.
      c.   Sam ate the apple.
      d.   The apple was eaten by Sam.
      e.   A cow is in the yard.
      f.   There is a cow in the yard.
      g.   Bill appears to be smart.
      h.   I gave Sam a fish.

If the transformations accounting for these relations are abandoned, then some alternatives must be offered in their place. It is of some interest that all of the transformations rejected in the previous chapter are structure-preserving; cf. [54]. It has been noted that the base generates structures which are essentially identical to those resulting from the Passive rule. Thus, for example, (20a) and (20b) are essentially structurally identical.

(20) a.   The boy was eating by John.
      b.   The apple was eaten by John.

Thus, the Passive shifts the underlying subject into an object of preposition

131

slot and the object into the subject slot. A priori, this need not be the case. One could conceive of a rule yielding (21) as the result of Passive.

(21)   The apple John was eaten by.

Such a rule would create structures unlike those generated by base rules, and, in fact, it has been argued that such rules exist—Emonds' root transformations—but only under stringent conditions, namely, when the S under consideration is a root S. Since passives are found in all S's, it is no coincidence that they "preserve" structure. The structure-preserving hypothesis of [54] is the only attempt to explain these observations, but it seems to me that there is an alternative: passive phrases exhibit base-like structure because they are base structures, that is, generated directly by base rules. This result is the natural culmination of a trend which can be traced beginning with *Syntactic Structures* (or earlier in [32]), where passives derive from actives, continuing with [36], where the passive *by*-phrase becomes part of the deep structure of passives,[5] and [27], where passive *be en* becomes part of the underlying Aux of passives,[6] continuing with [40], where the Passive is broken down into two stages, and proceeding up to [24], where the agent NP is actually generated in postposed position, as suggested in [54]. It is a small step to the position advanced here, a step which appears to be dictated by the elimination of Equi-NP Deletion.[7]

Granted that passives are generated directly, it remains to relate them to corresponding actives. One approach would be to formulate a lexical redundancy rule taking a form quite similar to the Passive transformation itself. On the other hand, the idea of a rule which is approximately the inverse of Passive is not unattractive. I will now sketch out an approach incorporating inverse transformations, termed *G*-rules (genotype rules), which operate on base structures to yield more abstract structures which ultimately tend to resemble the classical deep structures of [36]. Lest the reader lose sight of the motivation for *G*-rules, let it be noted that there is no need for (16) in the alternative. The inverse passive can now be formulated as two *G*-rules:

(22)   NP–Postposing:

$$
\text{NP}-\left\{\begin{array}{l}\text{tense (M)}\\\text{to}\\\text{ing}\end{array}\right\}\ (\text{have-en})\ (\text{be ing})\ -\ \text{be en}\ -\ \text{V}\ -\ e\ -\ \text{X}
$$

$$
\begin{array}{llllllll}
1\ - & & 2 & & -\ 3 & -\ 4 & -\ 5 & -\ 6 \Longrightarrow \\
e\ - & & 2 & & -\ e & -\ 4 & -\ 1 & -\ 6
\end{array}
$$

132

NP–Preposing:

e – Aux	V	NP –	by	–	NP	–	X
1 –	2	– 3	–	4	–	5	$\Longrightarrow$
4 –	2	– e	–	e	–	5	

Derivations illustrative of these rules are provided below.

(23) a.   the apple tense be en eat by Sam $\Longrightarrow$

NP–Postposing

tense eat the apple by Sam $\Longrightarrow$ NP–Preposing

Sam tense eat the apple

   b.   Sam tense eat the apple   No *G*-rules apply.

The output of the *G*-rules for the passive (19c) and active (19b) generated by base rules is identical, and therefore they are related inasmuch as grammatical relations are defined at this abstract level of representation. Subcategorization restrictions are in general checked cyclically after all other *G*-rules have applied. Thus, although the following are generated by the base rules, they are subsequently marked as deviant, since part of the lexical characterization of *sleep* is [−_____NP].

(24) a.   Everyone slept the bed.
   b.   The bed was slept by everyone.

An immediate advantage of this approach is that sentences such as (25) can be generated without ad hoc theoretical elaboration (such as an Agent-Deletion transformation or dummy agent).[8]

(25) a.   The city was destroyed.
   b.   Many wars have been lost.
   c.   No country should be bombed.

Since the *by NP* phrase of the Passive is a PP, it is optional in the base, as are other PP's. Thus, (25a–c) can be generated without an agent, with the result that NP-Preposing will be inapplicable and the abstract representations will be subjectless. It is, after all, a fact that (25a–c) are subjectless and agentless.[9] I will return to the Passive below and illustrate its function in complex sentences.

There are additional transformations dismissed in section 5.4 which can now be formulated as *G*-rules. In particular, *there*-Insertion and Object-Shift are replaced by their inverses:

(26) *there*-Substitution:

there – Aux be – NP – X
1   –   2   – 4 – 5 $\implies$
4   –   2   – e – 5

Object-Postposing:

NP – Aux Cop A' (PP) (to V)* to V – e – X
1 –   2   – 3 – 4 $\implies$
e –   2   – 1 – 4

Thus, sentences with expletive *there* will be generated directly, as will sentences which traditionally result from Object-Shift (or Object-Deletion [96]). Representative *G*-derivations include the following:

(27) a. there tense be a cow in the yard $\implies$ *there*-Substitution
      a cow tense be in the yard
   b. Mary tense be easy to please $\implies$ Object-Postposing
      tense be easy to please Mary

In this way, we relate (19e) and (19f), since they will have identical abstract representations, and (19a) and (19b), since they will exhibit analogous grammatical relations.

Support for this analysis comes from the following (b) examples which are not generable in the framework advocated here.

(28) a. Some boys were doctors.
   b. *There were some boys doctors.

(29) a. An elephant was small.
   b. *There was an elephant small.

If *there*-Insertion is a transformation, it must be somehow formulated so as not to apply to (28a) and (29a) to yield the (b) correspondents. But there are independent grounds for blocking (28b) and (29b) on the basis of phrase structure, and these can be brought to bear under the assumption that expletive sentences are generated directly by phrase structure. Compare the following:

(30) a.   Those were boys.
       b.   *Those were boys doctors.

(31) a.   It was an elephant.
       b.   *It was an elephant small.

Clearly the phrase structure rules used to generate (30a) and (31a), but not (30b) and (31b), can be used to generate (28a) and (29a), but not (28b) and (29b). Thus, the evidence suggests that sentences with expletive *there* be generated directly.

Emonds confronted the problems illustrated by (28) by formulating *there*-Insertion as a structure-preserving rule. This work served as a catalyst for the arguments of Jenkins for generating expletive sentences directly (cf. [77]), whose analysis I am adopting here in broad outline, though I leave open the question of whether *there*-Substitution can also be eliminated in favor of a general analysis of the coreference properties of (28–31).

It is sometimes claimed that *there*-Insertion fails to distinguish between copula and aspectual *be* so that it applies to (32a) and (33a) to yield (32b) and (33b).

(32) a.   A cat was chasing a mouse.
       b.   There was a cat chasing a mouse.

(33) a.   A whooping crane was shot.
       b.   There was a whooping crane shot.

However Jenkins has argued that the *be* in all such (b)-like variants is indeed the copula. Thus, we find parallel constructions in (34).

(34) a.   That was not a coyote making that noise.
       b.   That was a sonata played in the wrong key.

These examples are ambiguous, the relevant interpretation being that in which *making that noise* and *played in the wrong key* are not in the scope of the NP dominating *a coyote* and *a sonata*. Again, phrase structure rules generating (34) can be used to generate (32b) and (33b). There is, in summary, some evidence supporting the conclusion, reached on independ-

135

ent grounds in the preceding section, that *there*-Insertion is not a transformation in the classical sense.[10] This in turn supports the VP hypothesis.

Returning now to Object-Postposing (26), it appears that this formulation is not an unnatural end product of developments beginning with Postal's attempt to preserve the abstract S in [126], Bresnan's elimination of the S in favor of VP in [19], and the Lasnik and Fiengo formulation as a deletion rule in [96].[11] Lasnik and Fiengo in their interesting paper derive (19a) from the following deep structure by deletion of the coreferential pronoun:

(35) $Mary_i$ is easy to please her_i

One question this analysis raises is the following: How is (36) to be blocked?

(36) *John is easy to please Mary.

Lasnik and Fiengo stipulate identity in such cases, working within the framework of [44]. Within the framework advocated here, (36) will be generated as a base structure, but will undergo the following *G*-derivation:

(37) John is easy to please Mary $\Longrightarrow$ Object-Postposing
      John is easy to please John Mary

Now the strict subcategorizational restriction on *please* is violated because it is lexically subcategorized to select a single object. Thus, (36) is marked as deviant, in spite of the fact that it receives a phonological interpretation.

As alternatives to the two rules of Raising dismissed in section 5.4, I offer the following *G*-rules.

(38) Object-Lowering:

$$X - V' - NP - VP - Y$$
$$1 - 2 - 3 - 4 - 5 \Longrightarrow$$
$$1 - 2 - e - 3+4 - 5$$

Subject-Lowering:

$$NP - Aux\ V'' \quad (PP) - VP - X$$
$$i - 2 \qquad\qquad - 3 - 4 \Longrightarrow$$
$$e - 2 \qquad\qquad - 1+3 - 4$$

The symbols V′ and V″ are informal cover symbols for the two classes of raising predicates and "+" is to be interpreted as daughter-adjunction. The operation of these rules will be illustrated for complex sentences as they interact with other G-rules. In the framework adopted here there is an inverse cycle which commences with the root S and works successively through more deeply embedded cyclic nodes. The major category VP is considered here to be a cyclic node, as in phonology [46]. Strict cyclicity is defined as in the standard theory.

Object-Lowering and Subject-Lowering can now be illustrated by the following complex G-derivations:

(39)   A tense be en believe by B [to have en be en see by C]
$$\Longrightarrow \quad \text{NP–Postposing}$$
S_1
tense believe A by B [to have en be en see by C]
$$\Longrightarrow \quad \text{NP–Preposing}$$
B tense believe A [to have en be en see by C]
$$\Longrightarrow \quad \text{Obj.-Lowering}$$
VP_2
B tense believe [A to have en be en see by C]
$$\Longrightarrow \quad \text{NP–Postposing}$$
B tense believe [to have en see A by C]
$$\Longrightarrow \quad \text{NP–Preposing}$$
B tense believe C to have en see A

(40)   A tense seem to me [to have en be en examine by B]
$$\Longrightarrow \quad \text{Subj.–Lowering}$$
S_1
tense seem to me [A to have en be en examine by B]
$$\Longrightarrow \quad \text{NP–Postposing}$$
VP_2
tense seem to me [to have en examine A by B]
$$\Longrightarrow \quad \text{NP–Preposing}$$
tense seem to me B to have en examine A

(41)   there tense appear [to be a rat in the house]
$$\Longrightarrow \quad \text{Subj.–Lowering}$$
S_1
tense appear [there to be a rat in the house]
$$\Longrightarrow \quad \textit{there}\text{-Substitution}$$

137

VP_2

tense appear [a rat to be in the house]

Turning now to the problem of examples such as *John wants to be examined by the doctor*, we may formulate a rule of Equi-NP Insertion.

(42) Equi-NP Insertion (Equi):

$$X - NP_i - (Aux \quad V) \, _{VP}[- \quad e - Aux \quad Y$$
$$1 - 2 - \quad\quad 3 \quad - 4 - \quad\quad 5 \implies$$
$$1 - 2 - \quad\quad 3 \quad - 2 - \quad\quad 5$$

This rule gives rise to derivations such as (43), accounting for otherwise "missing" subjects.

(43) $John_i$ tense want [to be en examine by the doctor] $\implies$ Equi
$John_i$ tense want [$John_i$ to be en examine by the doctor]
$\qquad\qquad\qquad\qquad\qquad\qquad\qquad \implies$ NP–Postposing
$John_i$ tense want [to examine $John_i$ by the doctor]
$\qquad\qquad\qquad\qquad\qquad\qquad\qquad \implies$ NP–Preposing
$John_i$ tense want [the doctor to examine $John_i$]

I assume that distinct indices are assigned to all fully specified NP's, that pronouns are generated by the base, and that anaphoric relations are expressed by interpretive rules. (Equi-NP–Insertion can be alternatively formulated to insert coreferential pronouns or variables.) Let us now consider how this approach accounts for Chomsky's *persuade/expect* distinction [36].[12]

(44) John expected Mary [to be en examine by the doctor]
$\qquad\qquad\qquad\qquad\qquad\qquad \implies$ Obj.–Lowering
John expected [Mary to be en examine by the doctor]
$\qquad\qquad\qquad\qquad\qquad\qquad \implies$ NP–Postposing
John expected [to examine Mary by the doctor]
$\qquad\qquad\qquad\qquad\qquad\qquad \implies$ NP–Preposing
John expected [the doctor to examine Mary]

(45) John persuaded $Mary_i$ [to be en examine by the doctor]
$\qquad\qquad\qquad\qquad\qquad\qquad\qquad \implies$ Equi

John persuaded Mary$_i$ [Mary$_i$ to be en examine by the doctor]
$$\Longrightarrow \quad \text{NP–Postposing}$$
John persuaded Mary$_i$ [to examine Mary$_i$ by the doctor]
$$\Longrightarrow \quad \text{NP–Preposing}$$
John persuaded Mary$_i$ [the doctor to examine Mary$_i$]

6.3 THE STRATIFIED CYCLE VS. THE INVERSE CYCLE AND THE FILTERING PROBLEM

We now seek grounds for empirically distinguishing the stratified cycle and the inverse cycle. In this section I will briefly enumerate some of the points which lead me to consider the inverse cycle as a promising alternative to the stratified cycle.

In the first place, the inverse cycle allows for the gap in phrase structure to be filled, thus eliminating point (vi) of (16) altogether. That is, VP complements will be generated in phrase structure under the inverse cycle hypothesis.

Second, there is apparently no reason for a rule of pruning under the inverse cycle, so that point (v) of (16) is also eliminable. Recall that these two points were the sole remaining objections to the Stratified Cycle Hypothesis of the original list. None of the objections apply to the inverse cycle.

A third advantage of the inverse cycle was mentioned in the previous section: there is no need for a rule deleting abstract agents. Indeed, there is no need for abstract agents.

A fourth reason for favoring the inverse cycle concerns verb/particle constructions in English. In an important paper, Emonds [56] has argued that Particle-Hopping should not be formulated as a rightward movement rule, as is customary, but rather as a leftward movement rule. Emonds argues that the so-called particles are in fact prepositions and, hence, prepositional phrases. His distributional evidence is certainly suggestive. Thus, *John looked up the man* (under a verb/particle interpretation) derives from *John looked the man up* within Emonds' framework, where *John looked the man up* derives from *John looked up the man* within the standard framework. Emonds notes a potential objection to his ''inverse'' analysis of particles in English. Since verb/particle constructions are often taken to be lexical, the inverse analysis would imply discontinuous lexical items in deep structure.

> One might ask if the idiosyncratic verb-particle combinations . . .
> should not be contiguous in deep structure; this would have to be the
> case if lexical entries, viewed as insertion transformations, are con-
> strained to insert only continuous sequences into trees generated by
> the phrase structure rules. [56: 75]

Notice that this objection does not apply to the inverse cycle.[13] Lexical
insertion is not constrained as in the standard theory; rather, lexical co-
occurrence restrictions are checked inverse cyclically—in particular, after
leftward particle (or PP) hopping. Thus, the verb and particle will in fact be
contiguous at the point at which lexical subcategorization is checked.
Although lexical items such as *look up* will be generated discontinuously
by base rules, they will in fact be contiguous after the *G*-rules have
applied.[14]

Fifth, and finally, it appears that the inverse cycle provides a potential
solution to the filtering problem mentioned in section 5.2 of the preceding
chapter. The filtering problem was initially raised in connection with
relative caluses. The problem is to avoid generating relative clauses in
which there is no NP identical to the head of the clause. Thus, Chomsky
[36] sought to block examples such as (46) by recourse to boundaries as
discussed in 5.2.

(46) a. *John saw the boy who Mary likes the girl.
      b. *John saw the boy who Mary yawned.

Now a similar problem was mentioned in the previous section in connection with Object-Shift as reformulated by Lasnik and Fiengo. How do we
avoid generating (47)?

(47) *Mary is easy to please John.

The solution to this dilemma provided in the previous section can now be
summoned to explain (46) as well. I will assume that S can be expanded as
Comp S and that NP can be expanded as NP S. Thus, relative clauses
assume a [NP [Comp S $]_S]_{NP}$ configuration, whereas yes/no questions
assume a [Comp S$]_S$ configuration. It is further assumed that Comp dominates relative pronouns such as *who, which,* etc. (among other items such
as complementizers *that,* etc.). I also assume that complementizers such as
relative pronouns, etc., are marked as coreferential with their heads and
checked for agreement. This process eliminates *the rock who, that who, he*

which, etc., while allowing *the rock which, that which, he who*, etc. The complementizing *wh*-words of questions and embedded questions will have no head. (It has been argued in [26] that ''free relatives'' have heads.) With this much said, it is possible to give a tentative formulation of Relativization and Question-Formation as a *G*-rule.

(48) Comp-Insertion:

$$\begin{array}{ccccccc}
\text{Comp} & - & \text{X} & - & e & - & \text{Y} \\
1 & - & 2 & - & 3 & - & 4 \implies \\
e & - & 2 & - & 1 & - & 4
\end{array}$$

This rule has the effect of inserting (or alternatively copying) the Comp into its associated clause. The A-over-A principle, Bresnan's Fixed Subject Constraint [24], etc., can be stated as the inverse of current formulations. As an illustration of (48), consider the following:

(49) John saw the boy$_i$ who$_i$ Mary likes $\implies$ Comp-Insertion
       John saw the boy$_i$ Mary likes who$_i$

(50) who(m) Mary tense will see $\implies$ Comp-Insertion
       Mary tense will see who(m)

Of course Subject-Aux Inversion and *do*-Support are not *G*-rules; they are formulated as in the standard theory.[15]

Now the question arises: How does (48) guarantee that the *wh*-word is inserted into the desired position? It does not. Rather, (48) can give rise to uninterpretable structures, but these will be disposed of by cyclic subcategorization as mentioned earlier. We now have at our disposal a potential solution to the filtering problem raised in [36: 137–38]. Consider the following derivation:

(51) John saw the boy$_i$ who$_i$ Mary yawned. $\implies$ Comp-Insertion
       John saw the boy$_i$ Mary yawned who$_i$

Since *yawn* is intransitive and marked [− _____ NP], this sentence constitutes a violation. Similar remarks now apply to the following example:

(52) John saw the boy$_i$ who$_i$ Mary likes the girl
                                          $\implies$ Comp-Insertion
       John saw the boy$_i$ Mary likes who$_i$ the girl

This sentence is in violation of the subcategorizational restrictions on the verb *like,* which does not select more than a single object. The base structure in (51) is in all essentials what is blocked in [36] by means of word boundaries; that approach was criticized in section 5.2 above. Regardless of how we apply (48) to this base structure, a violation ensues so that no word boundaries need be employed.[16]

If we assume that *wanna, hafta,* etc., are generated directly, as in [32], we can use this analysis to explain why (53a) and (54a) are not ambiguous, as opposed to their (b) counterparts.

(53) a. Who do you wanna leave?
      b. Who do you want to leave?

(54) a. That's the doctor who I hafta investigate.
      b. That's the doctor who I have to investigate.

If *wanna* and *hafta* are single words in base structures, Comp-Insertion cannot apply ambiguously to the (a) structures as it can to the (b) structures. That is, the Comp cannot come to intervene between *haf-* and *ta,* though it can between *have* and *to,* etc.

This analysis also appears to eliminate the necessity for a "shadow" pronoun or "trace" approach to relative clauses and movement, as in [115].[17]

Extraposition will look more like Emonds' Intraposition (cf. [54], [8]), except that both of the following will be generated directly:

(55) a. It surprises me that John left.
      b. That John left surprises me.

Only the first example will undergo *G*-rule (56) to yield an abstract structure identical to (55a).

(56) Intraposition: it $-$ Aux V($\left\{\begin{matrix} PP \\ NP \end{matrix}\right\}$) $-$ $\left\{\begin{matrix} S \\ VP \end{matrix}\right\}$

$$
\begin{array}{ccccc}
1 & - & 2 & - & 3 \implies \\
3 & - & 2 & - & e
\end{array}
$$

Examples such as *that we are sixty percent water proves that we came from the ocean* and *that the night is black demonstrates that the universe is expanding* are not problematical; they do not undergo (56).[18]

A more complex derivation is illustrated by the final example:

(57)　it is obvious that it would be nice to win ⟹
　　　that it would be nice to win is obvious ⟹
　　　that to win would be nice is obvious

In conclusion, it appears that the inverse cycle does offer some promise. This suggests that it may be worthwhile to pursue the inverse cycle with deeper analyses than could be provided here.

NOTES TO CHAPTER 6

†*Note added in proof.* Still a third alternative, one which preserves the standard transformations but incorporates cyclic lexical insertion, was brought to my attention too late to permit discussion here. This alternative has been arrived at independently by Seegmiller [149], Evers [59], and perhaps others.

[1]Some evidence against this ''promotion'' analysis of relative clauses is provided in [26]. For more on the promotion analysis, see [147] and unpublished work of J.-R. Vergnaud.

[2]See, for example, Chomsky [41: fn. 28].

[3]The *make headway* example was first brought to my attention by Joe Emonds in connection with the passive. Its relevance to Relative-Clause–Formation is original with the author.

[4]*E*-rules should not be confused with the generalized transformations of [33], although clearly there is a striking similarity.

[5]Chomsky's arguments for *by Passive* can be found in [36: 104] and some criticism is provided in [90: 156–57, 164–65].

[6]In other words, Aux is expanded as (i):

(i)　Aux　→　tense　(M) (have en) (being) (been)

Here *be en* is the passive auxiliary inserted by the passive transformation of [33]. It is certainly not a coincidence that passive *be en* fits so conveniently into the auxiliary slot, a fact missed by the original analysis. The introduction of *be en* into phrase structure should perhaps be credited to Chomsky [36], where Aux is expanded as *tense (M) (Aspect).* Since no rule is given for expanding *Aspect,* it is unclear whether *be en* was intended as an expansion of *Aspect;* however, examples on p. 104 seem to argue against such an interpretation. It is particularly interesting that (i) is explicitly given by Chomsky in the earliest work on transformational grammar [32][33], where it is rejected for technical reasons.

[7]Emonds was the first to advocate generating passives directly in the generative framework (as early as 1968) before he adopted a structure-preserving framework, although much earlier in [32] Chomsky discussed the idea. Emonds also is credited with eliminating Equi-NP Deletion in [39] and [73], although he takes no position on this issue in [54].

[8]Recognition of the ad hoc nature of Agent-Deletion can be found in [58] along with a proposal for eliminating it.

[9]Some passives require agents and others must be agentless; cf. [8].

(i)   The fire was caused by a defective circuit breaker.
        *The fire was caused.

(ii)   *John was rumored by Bill to be tall.
        John was rumored to be tall.

[10]Emonds [54] is the first to attempt to come to grips with the problems raised by (10) and (11). He also notes the problem in the standard theory of ensuring that *there*-Insertion will apply to (i) to yield (ii):

(i)   *A war was.
(ii)   There was a war.

To Emonds' examples can be added the following:

(iii)   *But six boys are in the room.
        There are but six boys in the room.

(iv)   *Nothing is to the rumor.
        There is nothing to the rumor.

(v)   *Ever so much racket was in the corridor.
        There was ever so much racket in the corridor.

See also [85] for additional examples. More recently, Chomsky [45] has claimed that restrictions on what can follow existential *there* are semantic, citing unpublished work by Milsark to which I have no access. I am not sure what his position would be vis-à-vis restrictions on what cannot appear without *there* as in the examples cited in this note.

[11]Actually Ross [136] was the first to suggest the deletion analysis, although he subsequently abandoned it in [130], which in turn has subsequently been shown to be inconclusive by Akmajian in [1].

[12]I am assuming that Object-Lowering precedes Equi-NP Insertion, accounting for why Equi-NP Insertion does not apply to (44). It would be nice if Object-

Lowering could be eliminated altogether. At present I do not see a means of accomplishing this while at the same time distinguishing (44) and (45). Notice that *persuade* is not a lowering predicate, i.e., V′, and therefore (38) fails to apply to (45).

[13] Emonds himself attempts to overcome the objection by noting that there are discontinuous verb/PP idioms in English.

(i)   a.   John *took* his students *to task*.
       b.   *John *took to task* his students.

(ii)   a.   His proposal will *bring* the crisis *to a head*.
       b.   *His proposal will *bring to a head* the crisis.

Emonds claims that if the standard theory should insist on contiguous lexical insertion, then (ia) and (iia) must derive from (ib) and (iib) by an obligatory rightward PP-shift rule. If this is so, given such a rule, I do not see how Emonds overcomes the objection, assuming it is valid. On the other hand, I think there is an independent reason for the ungrammaticality of (ib and iib) having to do with the fact that no V PP NP construction is acceptable when the NP is not long enough. Thus, *John gave to Mary a dime* is also out, although *John gave to Mary a dime that his grandfather had given him* is perfectly acceptable, as is *John took to task the students who had been advocating unorthodox ideas.* Perhaps better examples for Emonds' case would have been the following:

(iii)   a.   The referee brought the boxer to.
       b.   *The referee brought to the boxer.
       c.   *The referee brought to the boxer who was downed by a hard left.

(iv)   a.   The doctor pulled the patient through.
       b.   *The doctor pulled through the patient.
       c.   *The doctor pulled through the patient who suffered acute priapism.

Blocking (iiib,c) and (ivb,c) remains a problem in the theory being discussed here, and in any theory for that matter. They may indicate that lexical contiguity is not feasible in all cases.

[14] Note that I am not claiming that all particle/NP constructions derive from NP/particle constructions, but rather that all NP/particle constructions generated by the base undergo the leftward particle (or PP) hopping transformation. In fact, I consider the base to also generate particle/NP constructions directly. Thus, *John looked Mary up* derives from *John looked Mary up* and *John looked up Mary* derives from *John looked up Mary.* Only at the level of analysis at which co-occurrence relations are checked will both be represented as *John looked up Mary.*

[15]Such rules I call *P*-rules (phenotype rules). To generate subject-Aux inverted sentences directly would entail a proliferation of phrase structure rules and is therefore to be avoided. The possibility of eliminating phrase structure rules altogether in favor of a recognition device with inverse transformations has never been considered. Such a device would presumably build structure and operate on it. It may be worthwhile to pursue such a program.

[16]It is sometimes assumed that relative clauses originate in the determiner and move to the right of their head by a special rule. This assumption is based on the co-occurrence restrictions that hold between determiner and relative clause. In the framework advocated here, relative clauses can originate to the right of the head and be inserted into the determiner by a *G*-rule, since co-occurrence restrictions are checked cyclically.

In a detailed and tightly argued paper, Bresnan [25] remarks, "Several puzzles posed by the comparative clause construction as a whole can now be solved, given one basic assumption: something in the clause is always deleted under 'identity with' (nondistinctness from) the head." It is not clear how this assumption is to be guaranteed, but her results would persist under a different assumption: instead of deletion in comparative clauses, we have insertion or copying of the relevant material. Such an approach could conceivably provide a unified solution to the "filtering problem" (relative clauses, comparative clauses, Object-Shift clauses). (There remain many questions of Comp interpretation for comparatives.)

An alternative to (48) would be to insert the heads themselves into their associated clauses.

[17]One difficulty with Perlmutter's analysis is that no rules are formulated to provide a basis for comparison. I do not have access to recent unpublished work cited in [45] which develops a "trace" theory of movement, so I am unable to determine whether a *G*-rule formulation could replace it. My suspicion is that this matter will be worth pursuing. It is also worthwhile to reconsider the arguments for a transformational (*P*-rule) approach to Quantifier-Postposition as in [51], [81], (and Quantifier-Movement) against the background of a *G*-rule formulation. For example, Dougherty notes that the ill-formedness of (i) would follow from the ill-formedness of (ii) if the former derived from the latter by Quantifier-Postposition.

(i)   The men both will meet in Altoona.
(ii)   Both of the men will meet in Altoona.

But clearly the same results are obtained under the assumption that both (i) and (ii) are generated directly and that by a quantifier-preposing *G*-rule, (i) becomes (ii), giving an identical selectional violation. Similar remarks apply to others of Dougherty's arguments. For example, he cites the following examples:

146

(iii)   Each of the men will hit the boy.
(iv)   The men will each hit the boy.
(v)   The boy will be hit by each of the men.
(vi)   *The boy will each be hit by the men.

and remarks: "Suppose that sentences [(iii) and (iv)] were generated as deep structures." "Then the Passive Transformation would require some ad hoc constraint to allow [(v)] to be derived from [(iii)], but to block deriving [(vi)] from [(iv)]." The ad hoc constraint can easily be averted in the framework adopted here by simply ordering the quantifier fronting rules before NP-Postposing and NP-Preposing. This yields a violation in the case of (vi).

[18] However the problem of blocking *that John left seems in base structures may indicate that Intraposition should be formulated as an indexing rule rather than a movement rule.

REFERENCES

1. Akmajian, A. 1972. Getting tough. *Linguistic Inquiry* 3: 373–77.

2. Anderson, S. 1970. On the linguistic status of the performative/constative distinction. NSF Report No. 26, Computation Laboratory of Harvard University, Cambridge, Mass.

3. ———. 1971. On the role of deep structure in semantic interpretation. *Foundations of Language* 7: 387–96.

4. Andrews, A. 1971. Case agreement of predicate modifiers in Ancient Greek. *Linguistic Inquiry* 2: 127–51.

5. Bach, E. 1968. Nouns and noun phrases. In *Universals in Linguistic Theory*, E. Bach and R. T. Harms, eds. New York: Holt, Rinehart, and Winston.

6. Bach, E. and Harms, R. T., eds. 1968. *Universals in Linguistic Theory*. New York: Holt, Rinehart, and Winston.

7. Baker, C. L. 1971. Stress level and auxiliary behavior in English. *Linguistic Inquiry* 2: 167–81.

8. Baker, C. L. and Brame, M. K. 1972. 'Global rules': a rejoinder. *Language* 48: 51–77.

9. Barone, J. M. 1972. A case of global rule incompatibility. *Papers in Linguistics* 5: 159–82.

10. Berman, A. 1973. A constraint on tough-movement. *Papers from the Ninth Regional Meeting*. Chicago, Ill.: Chicago Linguistics Society.

11. ———. 1974. On the VSO hypothesis. *Linguistic Inquiry* 5: 1–37.

12. Berman, A. and Szamosi, M. 1972. Observations on sentential stress. *Language* 48: 304–25.

13. Bowers, J. 1970. A note on 'remind'. *Linguistic Inquiry* 1: 559–60.

14. Brame, M. K. 1967. A new analysis of the relative clause: evidence for an interpretive theory. Unpublished ms.

15. ———. 1974. The cycle in phonology: stress in Palestinian, Maltese, and Spanish. *Linguistic Inquiry* 5: 39–60.

16. ———. 1975. Alternatives to the tensed S and Specified Subject Conditions. Unpublished ms., University of Washington, Seattle.

17.   Bresnan, J. W. 1969. On instrumental adverbs and the concept of deep structure. Quarterly Progress Report No. 92, Research Laboratory of Electronics, MIT, Cambridge, Mass.

18.   ———. 1970. An argument against pronominalization. *Linguistic Inquiry* 1: 122–23.

19.   ———. 1971. Sentence stress and syntactic transformations. *Language* 47: 257–81. Reprinted in *Contributions to Generative Phonology*, M. K. Brame, ed. Austin, Tex.: University of Texas Press. Also in *Approaches to Natural Language: Proceedings of the 1970 Stanford Workshop on Grammar and Semantics*, K. J. J. Hintikka et al., eds. Dordrecht, Holland: D. Reidel Publishing Co.

20.   ———. 1971. A note on the notion 'identity of sense anaphora'. *Linguistic Inquiry* 2: 589–97.

21.   ———. 1971. Contraction and the transformational cycle. Unpublished ms., MIT.

22.   ———. 1971. On 'A non-source for comparatives'. *Linguistic Inquiry* 2: 117–24.

23.   ———. 1972. Stress and syntax: a reply. *Language* 48, 326–42.

24.   ———. 1972. Theory of complementation in English syntax. Doctoral dissertation, MIT.

25.   ———. 1973. Syntax of the comparative clause construction in English. *Linguistic Inquiry* 4: 275–343.

26.   ———. 1975. Headless relatives. To appear in *Linguistic Analysis*.

27.   Burt, M. K. 1971. *From Deep to Surface Structure: An Introduction to Transformational Syntax*. New York: Harper & Row.

28.   Carden, G. 1968. English quantifiers. NSF Report No. 20, Computation Laboratory of Harvard University, Cambridge, Mass.

29.   ———. 1973. *English Quantifiers*. Tokyo: Taishukan Publishing Co.

30.   Chiba, S. 1972. Another case for 'Relative clause formation is a copying rule', *Studies in English Linguistics* 1: 1–12 (Asahi Press, Tokyo).

31.   Chomsky, N. 1951. Morphophonemics of modern Hebrew. Master's thesis, University of Pennsylvania.

32.   ———. 1955. The logical structure of linguistic theory. Unpublished ms., MIT Library.

33.   ———. 1957. *Syntactic Structures*. The Hague: Mouton.

34.   ———. 1962. The logical basis of linguistic theory. In *Proceedings of the Ninth International Congress of Linguists*, 1964, H. G. Lunt, ed. The Hague: Mouton. Revised as *Current Issues in Linguistic Theory*, 1964. The Hague: Mouton.

35. ———. 1964. *Current Issues in Linguistic Theory.* The Hague: Mouton.

36. ———. 1965. *Aspects of the Theory of Syntax.* Cambridge, Mass.: MIT Press.

37. ———. 1967. The formal nature of language. In *Biological Foundations of Language,* E. H. Lenneberg, ed. New York: Wiley. Reprinted in *Language and Mind,* Enlarged edition, N. Chomsky, 1972. New York: Harcourt Brace Jovanovich.

38. ———. 1967. Some general properties of phonological rules. *Language* 43: 102–28.

39. ———. 1968. *Language and Mind.* New York: Harcourt, Brace & World. Enlarged edition, 1972. New York: Harcourt Brace Jovanovich.

40. ———. 1970. Remarks on nominalization. In *Readings in English Transformational Grammar,* R. A. Jacobs and P. S. Rosenbaum, eds. Waltham, Mass.: Ginn. Reprinted in *Studies on Semantics in Generative Grammar,* N. Chomsky, 1972. The Hague: Mouton. (Original ms. written 1967.)

41. ———. 1970. Deep structure, surface structure, and semantic interpretation. In *Studies in Oriental and General Linguistics.* Tokyo: TEC Corporation for Language and Educational Research. Reprinted in *Semantics: An Interdisciplinary Reader in Philosophy, Linguistics and Psychology,* D. D. Steinberg and L. A. Jakobovits, eds., 1971. London: Cambridge University Press. Also reprinted in *Studies on Semantics in Generative Grammar,* N. Chomsky, 1972. The Hague: Mouton.

42. ———. 1972. Some empirical issues in the theory of transformational grammar. In *Goals of Linguistic Theory,* S. Peters, ed., 1972. Englewood Cliffs, N. J.: Prentice-Hall. Reprinted in *Studies on Semantics in Generative Grammar,* N. Chomsky, 1972. The Hague: Mouton.

43. ———. 1972. *Studies on Semantics in Generative Grammar.* The Hague: Mouton.

44. ———. 1973. Conditions on transformations. In *A Festschrift for Morris Halle,* S. R. Anderson and P. Kiparsky, eds. New York: Holt, Rinehart, and Winston.

45. ———. 1975. Questions on form and interpretation. *Linguistic Analysis* 1: 75–109.

46. Chomsky, N. and Halle, M. 1968. *The Sound Pattern of English.* New York: Harper & Row.

47. Cruse, D. A. 1972. A note on English causatives. *Linguistic Inquiry* 3: 520–28.

48. Culicover, P. W. 1974. An invalid evaluation metric. Social Sciences Working Paper 61, University of California, Irvine.

49. Davidson, D. 1966. The logical form of action sentences. In *The Logic of Decision and Action*, N. Rescher, ed. Pittsburgh, Pa.: University of Pittsburgh Press.

50. Dougherty, R. C. 1969. An interpretive theory of pronominal reference. *Foundations of Language* 5: 488–519.

51. ———. 1970. A grammar of coordinate conjoined structures I. *Language* 46: 850–98.

52. ———. 1973. A survey of linguistic methods and arguments. *Foundations of Language* 10: 423–90.

53. ———. 1973. Generative semantics: a Bloomfieldian counterrevolution. Unpublished ms.

54. Emonds, J. E. 1970. Root and structure-preserving transformations. Doctoral dissertation, MIT.

55. ———. 1972. A reformulation of certain syntactic transformations. In *Goals of Linguistic Theory*, S. Peters, ed., 1972. Englewood Cliffs, N. J.: Prentice-Hall.

56. ———. 1972. Evidence that indirect object movement is a structure-preserving rule. *Foundations of Language* 8: 546–61. Also in [66].

57. ———. 1973. Alternatives to global constraints. *Glossa* 7: 39–62.

58. ———. (in press). *A Transformational Approach to English Syntax: Root, Local, and Structure-Preserving Transformations*. New York: Academic Press.

59. Evers, A. 1975. *The Transformational Cycle in Dutch and German*. Doctoral dissertation, University of Utrecht.

60. Fillmore, C. J. and Langendoen, D. T., eds. 1971. *Studies in Linguistic Semantics*. New York: Holt, Rinehart, and Winston.

61. Fodor, J. A. 1970. Three reasons for not deriving 'kill' from 'cause to die'. *Linguistic Inquiry* 1: 429–38.

62. Fodor, J. Dean. 1974. Like subject verbs and causal clauses in English. *Journal of Linguistics* 10: 95–110.

63. Fodor, J. A. and Katz, J. J., eds. 1964. *The Structure of Language: Readings in the Philosophy of Language*. Englewood Cliffs, N. J.: Prentice-Hall.

64. Fraser, B. 1974. An examination of the performative analysis. *Papers in Linguistics* 7: 1–40.

65. Grinder, J. and Postal, P. M. 1971. Missing antecedents. *Linguistic Inquiry* 2: 269–312.

66. Gross, M., Halle, M., and Schützenberger, M.-P., eds. 1973. *The Formal Analysis of Natural Languages*. The Hague: Mouton.

67. Hall, B. [Partee, B. H.] 1965. Subject and object in modern English. Doctoral dissertation, MIT.

68. Hankamer, J. 1973. Unacceptable ambiguity. *Linguistic Inquiry* 4: 17–68.

69. Hasegawa, K. 1972. Transformations and semantic interpretation. *Linguistic Inquiry* 3: 141–59.

70. Helke, M. 1970. Reflexives in English. Doctoral dissertation, MIT.

71. Hust, J. 1975. Dissuaded. *Linguistic Analysis* 1: 173–89.

72. Ioup, G. 1975. The treatment of quantifier scope in a transformational grammar. Doctoral dissertation, CUNY.

73. Jackendoff, R. S. 1968. Speculations on presentences and determiners. Unpublished ms., distributed by Indiana University Linguistics Club, Bloomington, Ind.

74. ———. 1971. On some questionable arguments about quantifiers and negation. *Language* 47: 282–97.

75. ———. 1972. *Semantic Interpretation in Generative Grammar*. Cambridge, Mass.: MIT Press.

76. Jacobs, R. A. and Rosenbaum, P. S., eds. 1970. *Readings in English Transformational Grammar*. Waltham, Mass.: Ginn.

77. Jenkins, L. 1972. Modality in English syntax. Doctoral dissertation, MIT, distributed by Indiana University Linguistics Club, Bloomington, Ind.

78. Katz, J. J. and Bever, T. 1974. The empiricist nature of generative semantics. Unpublished ms.

79. Katz, J. J. and Fodor, J. A. 1963. The structure of a semantic theory. *Language* 39: 170–210. Reprinted in *The Structure of Language: Readings in the Philosophy of Language*, J. A. Fodor and J. J. Katz, eds., 1964. Englewood Cliffs, N. J.: Prentice-Hall.

80. Katz, J. J. and Postal, P. M. 1964. *An Integrated Theory of Linguistic Descriptions*. Cambridge, Mass.: MIT Press.

81. Kayne, R. S. 1969. The transformational cycle in French syntax. Doctoral dissertation, MIT.

82. Kimball, J. 1970. 'Remind' remains. *Linguistics Inquiry* 1: 511–23.

83. King, H. V. 1970. On blocking the rules for contraction in English. *Linguistic Inquiry* 1: 134–36.

84. Kisseberth, C. W. 1973. Is rule ordering necessary in phonology? In *Issues in Linguistics*, B. B. Kachru et al., eds. Urbana, Ill.: University of Illinois Press.

85. Kuno, S. 1972. The position of locatives in existential sentences. *Linguistic Inquiry* 2: 333–78.

86. Lakoff, G. 1965. On the nature of syntactic irregularity. NSF Report No. 16, Computation Laboratory of Harvard University, Cambridge, Mass.

87. ———. 1968. Some verbs of change and causation. NSF Report No. 20, Computation Laboratory of Harvard University, Cambridge, Mass.

88. ———. 1968. Instrumental adverbs and the concept of deep structure. *Foundations of Language* 4: 4–29.

89. ———. 1969. On derivational constraints. In *Papers from the Fifth Regional Meeting of the Chicago Linguistics Society*. Chicago: Chicago Linguistic Society.

90. ———. 1970. *Irregularity in Syntax*. New York: Holt, Rinehart, and Winston.

91. ———. 1970. Global rules. *Language* 46: 627–39. Reprinted in *Semantic Syntax*, P. A. M. Seuren, ed., 1974. London: Oxford University Press.

92. ———. 1971. On generative semantics. In *Semantics: An Interdisciplinary Reader in Philosophy, Linguistics, and Psychology*, D. D. Steinberg and L. A. Jakobovits, eds. London: Cambridge University Press.

93. ———. 1972. The arbitrary basis of transformational grammar. *Language* 48: 76–87.

94. ———. 1973. The global nature of the nuclear stress rule. *Language* 49: 285–303.

95. Lakoff, G. and Ross, J. R. 1972. A note on anaphoric islands and causatives. *Linguistic Inquiry* 3: 121–25.

96. Lasnik, H. and Fiengo, R. 1974. Complement object deletion. *Linguistic Inquiry* 5: 535–71.

97. Leben, W. R. 1971. 'Remind' once more. *Linguistic Inquiry* 2: 419–20.

98. Lees, R. B. 1960. *The Grammar of English Nominalizations*. The Hague: Mouton.

99. ———. 1960. A multiply ambiguous adjectival construction in English. *Language* 36: 204–21.

100. Lunt, H. G., ed. 1964. *Proceedings of the Ninth International Congress of Linguists*. The Hague: Mouton.

101. MacLane, S. 1971. *Categories for the Working Mathematician*. New York: Springer-Verlag.

102. McCawley, J. 1967. The respective downfalls of deep structure and autonomous syntax. Paper read before the Linguistic Society of America, 1967, dittoed.

103. ———. 1968. Lexical insertion in a transformational grammar without

deep structures. In *Papers from the Fourth Regional Meeting of the Chicago Linguistic Society.* Chicago: Chicago Linguistic Society.

104. ———. 1968. The role of semantics in a grammar. In *Universals in Linguistic Theory,* E. Bach and R. T. Harms, eds. New York: Holt, Rinehart, and Winston.

105. ———. 1970. English as a VSO language. *Language* 46: 286–99. Reprinted with additions in *Semantic Syntax,* P. A. M. Seuren, ed., 1974. London: Oxford University Press.

106. ———. 1970. Where do noun phrases come from? In *Readings in English Transformational Grammar,* R. Jacobs and P. S. Rosenbaum, eds. Waltham, Mass.: Ginn.

107. ———. 1971. Tense and time reference in English. In *Studies in Linguistic Semantics,* C. J. Fillmore and D. T. Langendoen, eds. New York: Holt, Rinehart, and Winston.

108. Menger, K. 1960. A counterpart of Occam's Razor in pure and applied mathematics onotological uses. *Synthese* 12: 415–28.

109. Milsark, G. 1972. Re: Doubl-ing. *Linguistic Inquiry* 3: 542–49.

110. Newmeyer, F. J. 1969. The underlying structure of the begin-class verbs. In *Papers from the Fifth Regional Meeting of the Chicago Linguistic Society.* Chicago: Chicago Linguistic Society.

111. ———. 1969. On the alleged boundary between syntax and semantics. *Foundations of Language* 6: 178–86.

112. Partee, B. H. 1971. On the requirement that transformations preserve meaning. In *Studies in Linguistic Semantics,* C. J. Fillmore and D. T. Langendoen, eds. New York: Holt, Rinehart, and Winston.

113. Perlmutter, D. 1968. Deep and surface constraints in syntax. Doctoral dissertation, MIT. Published with deletions as *Deep and Surface Constraints in Syntax,* 1970. New York: Holt, Rinehart, and Winston.

114. ———. 1970. *Deep and Surface Constraints in Syntax.* New York: Holt, Rinehart, and Winston.

115. ———. 1972. Evidence for shadow pronouns in French relativization. In *Papers from the Relative Clause Festival.* Chicago: Chicago Linguistic Society.

116. Perry, T. 1973. On arguing for global rules. Unpublished ms, distributed by the Indiana University Linguistics Club.

117. Peters, [P.] S., [Jr.], ed. 1972. *Goals of Linguistic Theory.* Englewood Cliffs, N. J.: Prentice-Hall.

118. ———. 1973. On restricting deletion transformations. In *The Formal Analysis of Natural Languages,* M. Gross, et. al., eds. The Hague: Mouton.

119. Peters, P. S., Jr. and Ritchie, R. W. 1969. A note on the universal base hypothesis. *Journal of Linguistics* 5: 150–52.

120. Phelps, E. 1975. Iteration and disjunctive domains in phonology. *Linguistic Analysis* 1: 137–72.

121. Popper, K. R. 1963. *Conjectures and Refutations: The Growth of Scientific Knowledge*. New York: Harper & Row.

122. Postal, P. M. 1966. Review of *Grammar Discovery Procedures*. *International Journal of American Linguistics* 32: 93–98.

123. ———. 1966. Review of *Elements of General Linguistics*. *Foundations of Language* 2: 151–86.

124. ———. 1970. On the surface verb 'remind'. *Linguistic Inquiry* 1: 37–120. Reprinted in *Studies in Linguistic Semantics*. C. J. Fillmore and D. T. Langendoen, eds., 1971. New York: Holt, Rinehart, and Winston.

125. ———. 1970. On coreferential complement subject deletion. *Linguistic Inquiry* 1: 439–500.

126. ———. 1971. *Crossover Phenomena*. New York: Holt, Rinehart, and Winston.

127. ———. 1972. A global constraint on pronominalization. *Linguistic Inquiry* 3: 35–39.

128. ———. 1972. The best theory. In *Goals of Linguistic Theory*, S. Peters, ed., Englewood Cliffs, N. J.: Prentice-Hall.

129. ———. 1972. Some further limitations of interpretive theories of anaphora. *Linguistic Inquiry* 3: 349–71.

130. Postal, P. M. and Ross, J. R. 1971. Tough movement si, tough deletion no! *Linguistic Inquiry* 2: 544–46.

131. Quicoli, A. C. 1972. Aspects of Portuguese complementation. Doctoral dissertation, University of New York at Buffalo.

132. Reibel, D. A. and Schane, S. A., eds. 1969. *Modern Studies in English: Readings in Transformational Grammar*. Englewood Cliffs, N. J.: Prentice-Hall.

133. Ronat, M. 1972. A propos du verbe 'remind' selon P. M. Postal, la semantique generative: une réminiscence du structuralisme? *Studi Italiani di Linguistica Teorica ed Applicata* 2: 241–67.

134. Rosenbaum, P. S. 1967. Phrase structure principles of English complex sentence formation. *Journal of Linguistics* 3: 103–18. Reprinted in *Modern Studies in English: Readings in Transformational Grammar*, D. A. Reibel and S. A. Schane, eds., 1969. Englewood Cliffs, N. J.: Prentice-Hall.

135. ———. 1967. *The Grammar of English Predicate Complement Constructions*. Cambridge, Mass.: MIT Press.

136. Ross, J. R. Constraints on variables in syntax. Doctoral dissertation, MIT, distributed by Indiana University Linguistics Club.

137. ———. 1969. Auxiliaries as main verbs. In *Studies in Philosophical Linguistics*, Series One, W. Todd, ed. Carbondale, Ill.: Great Expectations Press.

138. ———. 1969. A proposed rule of tree-pruning. In *Modern Studies in English: Readings in Transformational Grammar*, D. A. Reibel and S. A. Schane, eds., Englewood Cliffs, N. J.: Prentice-Hall.

139. ———. 1970. Adjectives as noun phrases. In *Modern Studies in English: Readings in Transformational Grammar*, D. A. Reibel and S. A. Schane, eds. Englewood Cliffs, N. J.: Prentice-Hall.

140. ———. 1969. Guess who? In *Papers from the Fifth Regional Meeting of The Chicago Linguistic Society*. Chicago: Chicago Linguistic Society.

141. ———. 1970. On declarative sentences. In *Readings in English Transformational Grammar*, R. A. Jacobs and P. S. Rosenbaum, eds. Waltham, Mass.: Ginn.

142. ———. 1972. Doubl-ing. *Linguistic Inquiry* 3: 61–86.

143. Ross, J. R. and Perlmutter, D. 1970. A non-source for comparatives. *Linguistic Inquiry* 1: 127–28.

144. Ruwet, N. 1972. *Théorie syntaxique et syntaxe du français*. Paris: Editions du Seuil.

145. ———. 1973. *Introduction to Transformational Grammar*. North-Holland Publishing Co.

146. Schachter, P. 1973. On syntactic categories: a critique of Lakoff's "Adjectives and verbs," Ross's "Adjectives as noun phrases." and Bach's "Nouns and noun phrases." In *Critiques of Syntactic Studies II*, UCLA Papers in Linguistics, No. 4, P. Schachter and G. Bedell, eds. Los Angeles: UCLA Press.

147. ———. 1973. Focus and relativization. *Language* 49: 19–46.

148. Searle, J. 1972. Chomsky's revolution in linguistics. *New York Review of Books*, June 29.

149. Seegmiller, M.S. 1974. Lexical Insertion in a Transformational Grammar. Doctoral dissertation, NYU.

150. Selkirk, E. 1972. The phrase phonology of English and French. Doctoral dissertation, MIT.

151. Seuren, P. A. M. 1972. Autonomous versus semantic syntax. *Foundations of Language* 8: 237–65. Reprinted in *Semantic Syntax*, P. A. M. Seuren, ed., 1974. London: Oxford University Press.

152. ———., ed. 1974. *Semantic Syntax*. London: Oxford University Press.

153. Steinberg, D. D. and Jakobovits, L. A., eds. 1971. *Semantics: An Interdisciplinary Reader in Philosophy, Linguistics, and Psychology.* London: Cambridge University Press.

154. Smith, D. L. 1974. 'death' and how to 'bring it about'. *Papers in Linguistics* 7: 253–59.

155. Stillings, J. 1975. The formulation of gapping in English as evidence for variable types in syntactic transformations. *Linguistic Analysis* 1: 247–73.

156. Tisza, L. 1962. The logical structure of physics. *Synthese* 14: 110–13. Reprinted in *Boston Studies in the Philosophy of Science,* M. W. Wartofsky, ed. Dordrecht, Holland: D. Reidel.

157. Wang, W. S.-Y. 1964. Some syntactic rules for Mandarin. In *Proceedings of the Ninth International Congress of Linguists,* H. G. Lunt, ed. The Hague: Mouton.

Index